Cotton Grass

PRAISE FOR BART SUTTER

These poems take risks. They are wise. They restore your faith in the drumbeat of your own heart.

— Carol Connelly, *Minneapolis Star Tribune*

Bart's poetry is light years away (thank God) from postmodern tactics; one might even say his aesthetic is pre-modern. There are many poems with rhyme and meter, an unabashed celebration of nature, and most amazingly, a healthy sampling of what we see little of these days: the affirmative poem."

— Stephen Dunn

Poetry of great skill, power, and beauty . . . What one starts to understand is that Sutter has both an eye and an ear: the poem's images are selected with telling exactitude, its rhymes are connective but unobtrusive, and its powerful, varied rhythms are controlled with masterful finesse and precision.

— Richard Simpson, *Tar River Poetry*

With roots in the ancient, Sutter is fireside storyteller, celebrant of lives, master of dirge and joke. And always he loves to make connections: past and present, love and wilderness, even thistle and Ted Hughes, who sets for Sutter an important standard—unapologetic strength.

— Philip Dacey

Barton Sutter is so thoroughly a Minnesota Scandinavian— with the usual streak of curmudgeonly pessimism—that he becomes something larger, a type of American artist and culture maker, an emblem of us at our best.

— Bill Holm

Cotton Grass

New and Selected Poems

of the North

(1977 – 2024)

Bart Sutter

NODIN PRESS

Cover art: Dorothea Diver
Cover design: John Toren
Author Photo: Tom Vaughan

Library of Congress Control Number: 2024935476

9 8 7 6 5 4 3 2 1

ISBN: 978-1-947237-57-5

Published by
Nodin Press
210 Edge Place,
Minneapolis, MN 55418
www.nodinpress.com

Printed in USA

For Dorothea

I'm driving north, my favorite direction,
But doubly so since it brought me to you.

Also by Bart Sutter

Poetry
So Surprised to Find You Here
Nordic Accordion: Poems in a Scandinavian Mood
Chester Creek Ravine: Haiku
The Reindeer Camps and Other Poems
Farewell to the Starlight in Whiskey
The Book of Names: New and Selected Poems
Pine Creek Parish Hall and Other Poems
Cedarhome

Fiction
My Father's War and Other Stories

Essays
Cold Comfort: Life at the Top of the Map

Contents

from

Farewell to the Starlight in Whiskey

(2004)

from

The Reindeer Camps and Other Poems

(2012)

from

Chester Creek Ravine

(2015)

New Poems

(2022-24)

... for there is a spirit in the woods.

– William Wordsworth, "Nutting"

Here is your water and your watering place.
Drink and be whole again beyond confusion.

– Robert Frost, "Directive"

from

Cedarhome

(1977)

Trying to Dream Up an Answer

Like a compass needle,
I keep coming back.
I can't explain the attraction,
Though I keep imagining this vein of ore
Turning to blood beneath a ridge
That would explain everything.

All morning, up to my neck in sunlight,
I have dozed in this clearing,
Trying to dream up an answer
To why I have come so far.
As if dreams told only the truth.
As if all these miles meant something.

And now this new question:
Why on earth has this butterfly
Chosen to light on my boot?

I Love Your Crazy Bones

Even your odds and ends.
I love your teeth, crazy bones,
Madcap knees and elbows.
Forearm and backhand
Hair makes you animal,
Rare among things.
The small of your back could pool rain
Into water a man might drink. Perfect,
From the whirlpools your fingers print
On everything you touch
To the moons on the nails of all ten toes
Rising and setting inside your shoes
Wherever you go.

What the Country Man Knows by Heart

1.
Why he lives there he can't say.
Silence is the rule.

But he knows where to look
When his wife is lost. He knows
Where the fish that get away go
And how to bring them back.
He's learned about lures
And knows how deep the bottom is.

He has been lost and found
Where he lives moss grows everywhere.
He's made his way home
The way gulls fly through fog,
Find where water turns to stone.

In country covered with trees
He can find the heartwood
That burns best.
He can find his wife in smoke.

He knows where to look for rain
And why the wives of city men
Cannot stop dreaming of water.

2.
When loons laugh, he does not;
He waits for what follows,
Feeling the meaning of animal speech
Crawl in the base of his brain.

But he knows there are no words
To answer the question the owl has kept
Asking all these years.

He knows a man alone
Will begin to talk to himself
And why at last he begins to answer.

3.
He would never say any of this.
He knows how often silence speaks
Better than words; he knows
Not to try to say as much.

But then he won't say, either,
How often he longs to break the rule,
How unspoken words writhe in his throat
And blood beats the walls of his heart.

Stalking the Wild Mushroom

Gourmet's roulette.
You need a guidebook
And lots of luck.

They are all in the same family:
Brothers to the frost
That jacks up the sidewalk,
Sisters to the terrible
Secrets of children.

They go up
Like tiny atomic bombs, something
Come near out of nothing
And going back again.
They must loom
Like water towers
To an ant, like shade trees
To a worm.

I find them
Beside an oxbow of old highway.
The freeway runs right by them,
Hissing like rain
In another world.

Those, disguised as clams,
Clinging to tree trunks
Like barnacles, are no good.
But these, tender, no bigger
Than the penises of three-year-olds,
Are good to eat. They feel
Much like the breasts of women.

I collect them. I take them home
And fry them alive. In the pan
They seem to complain,
And I murmur something
Comforting,
Something like "Mushroom,
Mushroom." I can't wait.
I put one where my mouth is
And think of elves.

Don't laugh.
It's a serious business.
People have died.

Cedarhome

1.
Make no mistake. The cedar
Is no weeping willow,
Has nothing to do
With women washing their hair.
What then? Hunchback? Gnome?
It isn't either. Whatever
Shape it assumes—pueblo ladder
Leaning into the skylight,
Upright as fire, crouched over
Like some dumb oversized
Bird that migrated into the muck
Of the early paleozoic—
Its feathery leaves are evergreen.
Cedar is a survivor.

It takes root
And stays root,
Becoming whatever it clings to.
It likes lakes and rivulets,
Swamps and sloughs, the dark beer
And winesap of things
Seeping back to ground zero.
It sucks them up, it lifts them from nothing
Up to its crown and leaves them there.
It wants wet, but, lacking that,
Can pass as a cold country cactus.
A patient, camel kind of plant,
Survive on blasted granite switchbacks.
Cedar is sinewy, tougher than we are.

The way cedar trees
Smell makes me think
Of things I like to drink:
Wellwater, gin, after-the-rain jasmine tea.

They smell like star anise,
They smell like the sea.
They are none of these.
Cedar is a thing in itself.

2.
Just learning to talk, I watched
My father's father shiver cedar shakes,
Slit them to splinters
With a flick of his jackknife,
Shave off curls, auburn, blond,
To kindle kitchen stove and furnace.
My mother kept her wedding dress
In a cedar chest to stave off
Moth and rot. She trusted cedar
With special treasures.
My father taught me to know one
When I saw one.

Cedar must be my relative.
Around it, I turn primitive.
I take one for my totem.
Why not? The tree has a worthy history.
In paintings by Zen masters,
They often appear, not quite there
In the mist. American Indians
Censed themselves with sage
And cedar. Swedes and Finns

Built saunas out of it
And whipped their wet bodies
Ruddy clean with greens of it.
Solomon beamed a temple
For the tribes of Israel
With the cedars of Lebanon.

3.
Can you believe it?
The Bible says, "Heaven
Lies north through the cedars."
I have doubted the word
But never the tree's
Fine facticity.

I once thought the twisted
Trunks perverted. And then one night
By firelight I saw the light:
The torque of the trunk tightens
In proportion to the persistence
With which it screws into muck and bedrock.
And the cedar's positive power
To retain and loose life after death
Proves, inversely,
The force of the process aforesaid,
Releasing, of course, the corollary:
To wit, death is only apparent,
Not nought.

How could I doubt it?
Hell, I was burning the evidence!
The deadfall I'd cut to the heart
Undid rivery ribbons of fire and smoke,

Streamers untwisting into the heavens.
What a warm, what an empirical proof!

The island I was on was adrift, a raft,
And the moon hung up
On a branch like a lantern. And then,
As if I needed a talking to,
A straggling line of geese,
A whole host of snows and blues,
Floated over, gaggling north.

4.
I didn't used to care much
What they did with me after I died.
Now I think I'd like to be planted
In a coffin knocked out of cedar planks.
What sweet seasoning that would be,
What a sloughing of flesh, what a mulch,
What peat-rich mouldering,
What lingering commingling,
What a cedarhome.

Daybreak

A goldeneye whistles across the lake,
And the dream breaks. I get up;
I go outside to see what's up.

It's one of those mornings:
No matter how softly I step,
I knock lichens off their perches,
Birds and animals disappear.

I walk to the water's edge and kneel,
Drink cold handfuls of my reflection.
When I am done, I am still there.

from

Pine Creek Parish Hall
and Other Poems

(1985)

Geneva

She was famous for kindness, Geneva.
And yet she could run down a hen
And chop off its head just like that.
"Macaroni!" I said, when I saw the insides,
And she crowed like a satisfied rooster.
I once watched her husband, the only man
I knew who had a mustache, string up
And slaughter a cow. I ran to Geneva
And buried my face in her lap. "Geneva,"
I said, "does it hurt?" "That old cow?"
Said Geneva. "Don't worry," she said.
"You don't feel a thing when you're dead."

Geneva giggled and taught me to piss
In the dark in a thunder jug.
I was from town and embarrassed,
But Geneva enjoyed that noise.
She taught me itchweed and outhouse.
She spanked me and wiped my ass.
She was a good one, Geneva.
The world was a joke, and everyone said:
"She's a real card, that Geneva."

She had warts and a nose, Geneva,
And a twisted smile with teeth,
But she also had beautiful daughters.
Hay and fresh faces and breasts.
They could cook. The kitchen had pails,
And everyone drank from the dipper.
I can taste the tang of the tin
And smell that slop-bucket stink

And the fragrance of bread on the table.
She was always baking, Geneva.

She taught me the stars, Geneva.
It was night. In the garden.
She was giving us something again:
Carrots, cucumbers, tomatoes, and such,
Everything cool and slick. "Chicken shit,"
Said Geneva. "That's the secret," she said.
My pants were all wet with the dew.
"Look at that," said Geneva
And showed me the star-spangled sky.
"It's a coloring book," said Geneva.
"It's all dot-to-dot. Don't you see?"
And I saw: The Sisters, The Hunter,
The Bull and the Bear, The Dipper
From which we all drank.

So I thank the stars for Geneva,
All of her muscles and fat, that
Quick chicken-killer, that ugly
She of the beautiful daughters
And prize-winning hogs, that woman
Of pickles and jam. Geneva,
She taught me the mud and the stars,
And when I am ready to die,
She will come with her hatchet in hand
And her face like a kerosene lamp
And her dress all feathers and blood.

The Beaverhouse Downriver

In the old forever-never days
When I was blond and ten,
A beaver clan claimed the bend
Across the river. They badgered holes
And rumpus room, adobe dens
And chimney flues, spiral ramps and hatchways:
A complex, subterranean terrarium.
They chiseled and chewed
Through cottonwoods and poplars
As thick as cabin logs. With simple, secret
Principles of beaver mathematics,
They muscled timber down the bank
And built a barricade, an earthwork
Battlement of naked sticks
Plastered up and stuccoed
With pungent rivermuck.
They made the water sleep.
They littered the river with bittersweet
Aspen, alder, elder, willow
Chips and leaves and strips of juicy bark.

Behind a blind of willow slash,
The Wetzler boys and I stood watch
Until the trees grew together
And the early evening floodlight failed.
Then we caterwauled applause
That the beavers would return
With their crackshot tails.
We watched with sympathy half animal.
Full of the devil, there were days

We downed a tree ten times our age,
Lopped off limbs, bucked the trunk,
And peeled the green bark back
For fun, for no good reason
But the slippery feel of slick sapwood.
We were builders, too—constructed
Huts and forts and lean-to's, dugouts
To protect us from our enemies, adults
Who owned the world.
Everything the beavers did
They did without the help of men.

And so we loved them,
Savagely. Jimmy trapped one
With a steel-jaw, an underwater set
He'd read about. I forget
The fur, the teeth I should remember.
The tail was a thick, tough tongue—
Rough and cold, reptilian.
We talked of mountain men
Who ate them, and, after a day or two,
We threw the beaver back
In the black river where it belonged.

By late fall the moat froze.
We attacked the dam, pried loose
Dry deadwood, built bonfires.
Up to no good one day, we were
Nosing around their animal manholes
When something cracked
And Ken fell in.
We thought they'd kill him.
A crow cawed twice. Under ice,

The river groaned.
Then Ken called out: "Come on!
Nobody's home!"

Down under: dark and warm,
The quiet of a country church,
A bomb shelter without the war.
It was peaceful as a pantry, a cellar
Stocked with sedge and arrowhead,
Roots and tubers, baby potatoes, wild onion.
The floor had Oriental rugs:
Scattered mats of cattail, rush and reed.
There was sitting room, a sleeping ledge,
Nooks where we could range
Our pocketknives and precious stones.
And did. It was complicated,
The way we felt down there.

We went there daily. That hideaway
Was just what we wanted,
A wild retreat where we were free
To practice our religion:
Tobacco and women.
The smoke inspired angry guesses:
What were they, under their dresses?
Tits were tits, of course, but
Was it really gunt or was it cunt?
And was it true about the hair?
And did your father ever
Kiss your mother there?
Such talk. But mostly we just sat
Scared quiet, half-ecstatic, expecting
Some she-beaver to come

Barreling out of a burrow,
Terrible as a grizzly bear,
As good as God.

What happened? We never
Saw the beavers again.
Later a construction gang
Straightened out the river,
And, boys, we couldn't help it,
We kept on getting bigger,
And we moved away forever,
And all the grownups died.

The Berries

Wear a hat for the gnats and sun.
A long-sleeved shirt, though hot,
Will provide you some protection,
But your best defense is the oldest one,
And it's basically smack and swat.
Watch out for the prickly stem.
Keep telling yourself this is fun.
Though you dope yourself with repellant
And fan away flies with a branch,
There will be blood on your hands.
This is the secret ingredient,
The unwritten rule in the recipe,
The finder's fee you must pay:
A pound of flesh for a pint of jam.

The work will be sticky and warm
But not without certain rewards:
Flocks of flowers—red, white, and blue—
And fungus aglow on green logs,
The tropical cluck of a cuckoo,
Crows in the distance barking like dogs,
The heady incense of humus and ferns,
And the bright velvet thimbles,
Themselves. The red ones, the ripe ones
Resemble soft buttons and may be undone
With a gentle, pleasurable pull.
As you drop them into your pail,
You will hear an almost inaudible tune
That might be played on a vibraphone.

Once you have eaten your fill
And all your pots and pans are full,

Go home and heat up the kitchen.
Boil your berries with sugar and pectin,
Funnel the syrup in sterilized jars,
And top it all off with hot wax.
Wash up. Have a beer. And relax.
You've got Christmas gifts for the neighbors
And a bloodbank prepared for December.
One day you may open your cupboard
In search of a sweet transfusion
And be warmed by an infrared glow.
The itch of today's irritations
Will have healed a long time ago.

The Stallion

Walking the dry winter woods,
I reached the hidden pasture
And paused to admire the mare and stud
Till he came after me, the bastard.

He ran right at me, reared,
And whipped around to kick.
I hollered, "Hyah!" but he didn't hear,
So I retreated, throwing sticks.

He'd always been shy and mild,
But the mare was so fat with his foal
He'd suddenly grown wild,
Proud as a prince, powerful.

He chased me half a mile
Till I rolled beneath a fence.
He stood there sweating, male,
Magnificent. I dusted off my pants.

"So long," I said, "you son of a bitch."
And headed home. The sky was red and violet.
Reeds and cattails rattled in the ditch.
I felt a wonderful violence.

Witch Tree

Grown out of granite,
She's cut like a bowsprit

Through flurries of snow, fog, spray,
And simmering midsummer days.

She must take her moisture
Out of the air. There's no humus here—

Only a few fluorescent
Lichens that grow on the rock like rust.

Resisting the seasonal seesaw,
This tree supports ephemera.

At the moment a fritillary butterfly
Flickers around the roots, and high

Up the trunk a spider suspends a net,
A doily both deadly and delicate,

To fish for flies. This driftwood
Lives and, most lately, has withstood

Picture postcards, stupid verses,
Chippewa legends, the Chamber of Commerce.

So far, no vandals have dared
To carve initials here.

So God bless fear and superstition,
Whatever grants this tree protection.

They say she's a witch,
But she burns like a blowtorch,

Inhales the breath of animals,
Converts exhausted air to chlorophyl,

Gives off the oxygen
We breathe, and it begins again.

Biology may call this photosynthesis,
But, sitting here, I know that this is

Grandma, old and gnarled.
This is the light of the world.

November 7, 1984

"In every defeat are to be found the seeds of victory."
— Concession Speech, Fritz Mondale

Not one of my candidates won. Not one.
So I go for a walk in the woods,
Where I've gone for help since childhood.
Here you can howl like a wounded wolf
Or suck the slick bones of defeat
And who cares? Blasted tree trunks
And fallen limbs, ruin all around me,
Say, "Hey. It's a familiar story."
The leaves lie fading like wet confetti,
Like crepe paper streamers and broken balloons.

The lady who lives downstairs—
A tough old girl who farmed for years
And used to slaughter—wept last night.
"I must be getting old," she apologized.
"But if Reagan's elected, you might as well croak.
That's just how I feel." I felt numb.
She'd used up all the grief in the room,
So I took what was left and swore
And stomped and slammed some doors
While my wife sat still, struck dumb.

Now there's the scent of snow on the wind.
Crows boil up out of the oaks
Like smoke from a fire of rubber tires.
Sundown. Dark. I turn for home.
Home, I pour a few fingers of whiskey
And flick on the lights. Burn, baby, burn.

I've got a sizeable chip on my shoulder
And a cocklebur stuck to my collar
Like a political pin. My socks and sleeves
Bristle with stickers and seeds.

A Celebration of Rust

I am so weak my enemies
Have never even heard of me.
And even if they knew me, even if
I crashed their party,
They would smile on me
With contemptuous courtesy
While the goblets in their hands
Glittered like teeth. I speak
Of the take-charge guys,
The ones who own all the neckties,
And the women who wish they were men.

They don't even know who I am.
And why should they? I am
Nothing much, myself, so much dust,
But I do have powerful friends.
Termites, for instance, and ants,
The soft emery cloth of the wind,
Sandpaper snowstorms, and rain,
The mild acids of which
Will eventually etch their names
Off all the monuments
And melt down every memorial.

I have many powerful friends.
Frost may be my favorite,
But rust is one of the best
And the truest. Rust is the breath
That clouds the full-length mirror where
The men made of money admire themselves.
It takes years, but it will attack

Airplanes and tanks, banks and bridges
With equal indifference and win.

I take great satisfaction in rust.
It is patience in action
And powerful as the grass. Rain
Runs a bead which is welded by sunlight,
And red soot reduces blue steel
To a powder. A mineral amoeba,
Rust eats iron and multiplies
As furiously as a fungus. It deepens
Like humus, collecting and building
A fine film of metallic dust.

This is raw power. This is the cutting edge
Between here and there. It borders on air
And will finish the shiniest surface.
And when the buildings of the high and mighty
Have finally fallen and rest in ruins,
They will be blanketed with dried blood,
With rust, the loveliest pollen.

Hoarfrost and Fog

I walk six blocks to the park.
Hoarfrost and fog and ten below zero,
A full twelve inches of snow.
No one believes in the mysteries
Anymore, but still, once or twice
Every year this will happen:
Hoarfrost and fog and snow all at once.
I don't often notice my breath,
But here I am breathing and breathing.
And here is a kid in a scarlet parka,
Pulling a sled through the sugarbush.
He knew all along this would happen.
I forget, and yet once, maybe twice a year,
We enter this other kingdom. We're here.
And here is a woman so black
And slender and thin, I think of a statue
My friend brought back from Liberia.
She is wading around with a camera,
As if she could capture this hoarfrost
And fog that is softer than breath.
We smile. She hesitates, then decides
She will speak. She says, "Oh!
In my country where I come from
We have many amazing things,
But there, there is nothing like this!
I would like you if you take my picture?"
I fiddle with the little black box,
Back off, watch her smile and say,
"Can you fit all this everything
Inside the picture? Do you think it will show?"
"I don't know," I tell her. "I'll try."

My fingers are cold. The shutter is stiff,
But it clicks. The fruit tree behind her
Is heavy with frost, the apples are withered
But red. There is fog in the background,
The snow is nearly up to her knees.
I breathe, and I breathe, and I breathe.

Lost in *Antarctica*

If hell is hot, this must be heaven.
A mystic might have such a vision
Nearing death. These aren't pictures
Of the moon, Neptune, or Jupiter.
This is Earth, and it is strange.
On every page I'm rearranged
By the view that Porter's chosen
And alchemically flash-frozen.

This so far south of south
Every vantage point looks north.
The aerial shots cause vertigo.
I keep confusing rock with snow.
The ocean steams like smelting ore,
And the rubber seals along the shore
Are nothing compared to the penguins,
Which are birds but do not fly but swim.

This desert is home to animals
Who've somehow evolved without us,
Who live off the fat of the sea
And a couple of vague ideas.
Do they appreciate the sculpture
Everywhere, this rainbow-colored
Ice? Who knows? I suppose
They enjoy the way the wind blows.

A photograph of half a dog
Illustrates the gruesome logs
Of men who first explored this place
Like aliens from outer space.

The camera caught their biscuit cans
And oddly beautiful pots and pans.
In Shackleton's hut there's a frozen lunch
And a row of boots on a blue bench.
Porter took these in his seventies,
Transcending praise and envy.
The light looks hard as rock. This man
Braved the terrifying feminine
Force of water, snow, and loved it.
Here, and here again, we have it.
This is what it's like to earn your death,
To squint one eye and see the truth.

from

Farewell to the Starlight
in Whiskey

(2004)

The New Green

An overcast afternoon in mid-May.
The trunks of the aspens are silver today.
Tomorrow they might be olive or black,
But today they are silver. The leaves are lime-green,
As if lit from within. I love this new green,
So yellow and tender. I've loved it
Each year of my life, but never like now.
I'm driving north, my favorite direction,
But doubly so since it brought me to you.
The plum trees step out from the dark evergreens
And show off their blossoms. I love that fresh white.
I'm still too far south, but here in the car
I'm already there. Your daughters are sleeping.
We speak in hushed tones. I love your low voice.
The brandy is amber. Your eyes are light brown
And lit from within. You smile the smile
I survived all these years to discover. Oh, lover,
I love the crescent moon of your smile,
The curve of the road, the slope of your back,
The black of your hair, these black-and-blue rivers,
The buds of your breasts and the buds of these trees.
I'm very fond of the blonde and brown weeds,
But I love the love in your light brown eyes,
And now, more than ever, I love this new green.

Consider the Lilies

Consider the lilies of the lake.
Unlike the lilies of the field,
They have never heard of Jesus,
They are ignorant of Easter, and yet
Each year they resurrect themselves
Out of themselves, out of water and sunlight.
They show the water and the sunlight what they are.
They do not have the shape of trumpets,
They do not blare their beauty,
They only open slowly, like so many women.
Rising from the waters, they bare themselves
And shine, suspended in the waters.
Aroused by the wind, their wet leaves lift,
And their undersides show red.

They are purposeless, these lilies,
Though beavers fatten on their roots,
And the bull moose wades in among them
Right up to his beard and eats.
He raises his huge head, he grunts and blows,
Water runs off his jaws. His antlers,
Spread like the wings of an eagle, are tangled
With flowers and greens.

The lilies of the lake do not exist for us. They simply are.
You seldom see them from the road. They grow
In silence, unobserved, in shallow bays of northern lakes,
Guarded by the swords of spruce and tamarack.
And that's where we are now, my love. The lake is blue,
The sun is warm, and the wind that riffles waterlilies
Also rouses us. It cools us and carries

The aroma of the forest that makes us both feel drunk.
This is exactly where we've always longed to be—
Here, among the lilies, unafraid of thunderheads
Massed on the horizon. We will reach the shore,
Make camp, eat, love, and sleep
Right through the storm. If lightning strikes us,
We will die, but this will make no difference.
The white-throated sparrow will still sing at dawn,
And the smallmouth bass will break the surface.

You turn and smile at me from the bow
And point where you would have us go.
I stroke a lazy J in the water to correct our course—
A little J for Jesus or The Joker or for Joy—and we enter
The garden of liquid delights. Or is it
The other way round, and you are in the stern,
I'm up front, and it's your smile rather than the sun
That warms my back? I only know
The lilies part for us, the garden opens.
The leaves of the lilies whisper, and their blossoms
Drown beneath the bottom of our boat.
We glide on through in our silver canoe,
And, when we pass, the lilies rise again.
When we pass, the lilies of the lake close again behind us—
Undisturbed, eternal, fragrant, and calm.

The Boy Birch Tree

Lady of trees and flowers, you
Have planted a flowering tree in my name
And named me every tree and shrub
You started in your yard—working
From grief, fingers groping raw, cold earth,
Feeling your way toward some belief—
And walked me into the woods to find
The balm of Gilead, uncurling its new leaves,
The source of that sweet perfume
Which has haunted us all of our lives.
But for all of your generous energy,
I have worried about your daughters—
How I could help you raise them,
What blight I might inflict, how they might
Choke my own new growth, and, worst,
The wild jealousy you generate in us all.
But one bright afternoon you brought
Your girls and flowers and food.
And there in my own backyard, you found
The boy birch tree. "Look," you laughed,
"He's shedding his skin like a snake.
I love when they do this." You peeled away
A shred of old, brown, loose, translucent skin
To show the bright white bark below.
"See?" you said, and we laughed.
A small, unadulterated happiness.
At last, before you drove away, I saw
The look on your daughter's face as she looked
At the look on mine as I returned your gaze,
And I felt the sort of faith you feel
When you set a plant in the dark, moist ground,
Imagining green though the grass is brown.

Peregrine

In those days a decree went out
From the Stearns County Courthouse. I was free
To love you as I wanted, and I wanted you
With all my skin. That very weekend
We came together in a hotel room
Thirty stories high above the city
And saw how love was doubled
And redoubled in the floor to ceiling mirrors,
How our earthbound, mortal bodies
Came rushing forward from infinity
And exploded in that instant
When we shed our clothes and flew
Into each other's arms. There were mirrors
Everywhere in that high room
And out the window, too.
For when we rested from love's labor
And sat looking out, opposite,
Above the tallest building of the city,
We saw a peregrine
Sailing like a kite above the canyons.
As we watched the falcon flash and turn,
We hushed, and the flesh along our arms
Dimpled with excitement. And then the moment came.
Who knows how they know or how they have the gall to go?
Intuition must insist: *Do this now or die.*
The falcon folded his wings and dropped,
A living bomb, in his heart-stopping stoop,
One hundred eighty miles an hour headfirst toward
                    the pavement.
And then the opening of wings, the swoop,
The rising up, and all that open sky.

He might have gone right on like a bullet,
But he turned, then, and alighted
On a cornice of that manmade sandstone cliff,
Where he was greeted by his mate. We gasped,
And a thousand empty windows gaped
As the peregrine, who knew his mate,
His fate, what he was for, cried kyrie
From his aerie in the bright blue air
High above the city.

Night Fishing, Lake Polly

I spoke to nobody all day long
But the wind, my canoe, and a family of otters
Who chattered and hissed like my own.
Now I stand here on granite
And cast a white spoon at black water.
The slippery fish keep to themselves,
But the moon is afloat like a white waterlily,
And stars glint like stones at the bottom.

I talk to myself, that invisible being
Who haunts me most when I think I'm alone,
And I catch myself calling me *you*.
"You should quit fishing now.
You should head for bed soon."
Out here in this solitude smelling of cedars,
I seem to be both me and you,
And we are my father, my mother,
My lover, my brother, that ghost in the woods
Who sings in my blood, urging courage
And uncommon sense: "Everything breathes,
Even rocks."

        I cast for the island
But come up with nothing more than a glimpse
Of something that shimmers, then glimmers and grows,
Unrolling over the trees, a dragon of light,
Chinese. I am fishing for nothing
And land it again and again, nothing less
Than the northern lights and the moon,
Which is both high and dry, wetter than water,
And frosting the leaves of the trees,

As I know we are, too, both
What we are and are not, as I am
Living proof of this truth,
Standing on rock but feeling like water,
Filled with reflections but coming up empty,
Wildly happy here on Lake Polly,
Not catching walleyes and missing my wife,
Whose name is not Polly.

Milk

The anxious agony of raising kids
Drains the life from parents, who must grow
From cradling to tug of war to slowly letting go
And learn to live with worry till they're dead.
When I fell in with you, I felt both joy and dread
Because you came with two small girls in tow.
I said, "I do." I'm glad I did, even though
I sometimes feel I married them instead.

It helps me to recall that gauzy, green meadow
Where we saw a tawny fawn duck under
The belly of its watchful, patient mother
And deliver two hard headbutts to the doe,
Doing what it took to get the milk to flow.

Yardwork

Moldering leaves have clogged the drain,
So I clean the gutters in a pouring rain,
Then carry the ladder to the weathered shed,
Hunch on a stump, and shake out a smoke.
Raindrops dingle on the old tin roof.
For the moment, at least, I'm weatherproof
And backed by quarters of birch and oak,
Rakes and spades slung overhead,
A hose on a hook, an axe at hand,
A leaning tower of old paint cans.
Iris glitters, the lawn is lush,
And the years go by in a blurry rush.
The girls drive now, reject their bikes.
When was it we gave away their trikes?
Their sandbox blooms, a flowerbed.
The saplings you planted climb sky-high
As our parents whimper, groan, and cry.
I'm sheltered here by years of work,
Your deep green dream and the pains you took,
Building this tender hedge against death:
Flowering hawthorn and bridal wreath,
Forget-me-nots, lilacs, baby's breath.

Rose Hips

Observing this year's plump rose hips,
I thought of ovaries and your plush lips,
How pods will break, surrender seed,
And you crack open, moist with need.
A hummingbird arrived just then
And probed the blossoms one by one.
Those last few blooms were all but done.
Let's go back to bed again.

This

This thistle is magnificent,
Rising out of the sandy plain
Like a knight from the Middle Ages.
Tall as a man, it barely sways
In the wind that flusters the cottonwood trees
And flattens the grass on all sides.

This is the boy who bristled
Whenever his mother came near,
Who sent her away to the south
The same night he slaughtered his father.
Woe to his brother, tears and woe.
His brother's name is forbidden.
His sister fled long ago.

The pagan king of emptiness,
This thistle lords it over
Goatsbeard, milkweed, the tender,
Foolish flowers.
His virtue is courage, his vice is contempt.
His blades are edged with silver,
His spiky crown is stuck
With studs and purple gems.

Meaner than an ice pick,
This thistle stands on the sandy plain,
Glittering like shattered glass,
Glorious, barbaric.

In memoriam
Ted Hughes

Handyman

The morning brought such a lashing rain
I decided I might as well stay inside
And tackle those jobs that had multiplied
Like an old man's minor aches and pains.
I found a screw for the strikerplate,
Tightened the handle on the bathroom door,
Cleared the drain in the basement floor,
And straightened the hinge for the backyard gate.
Each task had been a nagging distraction,
An itch in the mind, a dangling thread;
Knocking a tiny brass brad on the head,
I felt an insane sense of satisfaction.
Then I heard a great crash in the yard.
The maple had fallen and smashed our car.

Cocklebur

Tossing trash branches down the ravine,
Avoiding their whiplash, cutting and mean,
I stooped way too low and tangled my hair
On a stickery, plump, fresh cocklebur.
My wife was amused and tore the bur out
While I bowed my head and swallowed a shout.
The little land urchin, that green porcupine
Had been waiting to snag a warm body like mine.
The plant meant no harm; it just had a need
For something with legs to carry its seed,
But I learned a lesson from nature's tomfoolery,
That nasty piece of vegetable jewelry.
I could sympathize with the mangiest cur,
Having got caught by my own patch of fur.

Fall Flowers

Sunflowers, primrose, butter-and-eggs,
These are the last of the gold.
Asters announce the annual disaster:
Our part of the planet turns cold.

Will we think of the snowflakes as flowers
So wild they'll never be sold?
Or will we grow dark and bitter
And wither before we are old?

Jack Pine

Oh, Jack Pine, I love you,
Even though you are dead,
Even though and even because
You aren't my kind and can't love me back.
God knows I've felt the same pointless affection
For women I've only gazed at across a room, to whom
I was never properly introduced
But went on loving wildly forever nevertheless.
Besides, I don't care what people call me
Anymore since anytime now, very soon,
I'll be a mumbling, daft old man
Like my father before me,
And then I'll be dead
Like my father before me,
So I might as well declare myself
Right here, clearly, while I can.

Jack Pine, I love you because
Your branches bend gracefully down toward the ground
Like the arms of a ballerina
In a certain modest position I can't name
But recognize at a glance, anywhere, even here,
Hundreds of miles from the nearest dance theatre.
Such poise. Such patient power. Brava! Bravissima!

Oh, I could say your drooping limbs
Resemble the down-curved wings of a bird
Protecting her brood, except you can't fly,
No matter how big the wind,
So that can't be right.

No, I see
I was more right before:
You're a woman, old woman, Jack Pine,
For your bare arms are bent,
Your skin has grown scales,
And you wear your tangle of twigs
Like a shawl of gray lace. Still,
Come sunset, your grace, you grow
Young once again, so dark and romantic I know
Your true name isn't Jack Pine, Jack Pine,
But must be Jacqueline.

Oh, Jacqueline,
Your silhouette is so naked,
So black and attractive against the afterglow
I can see clear through you to your future.
All your life long you have stood here
Patiently, rooted in rock, gripping
Your pairs of pine cones like little bells
That trembled in the wind and shook out
Their silent music for years on end.
For years on end, you have swayed here,
Dancing in place, stretching higher, higher,
Straining after something you knew not what
But felt in your very xylem and phloem
Would be your fulfillment—something
Like the sky, like the sun, something hot—
You knew not just what but felt
An overpowering desire to be opened,
To be ruined, to be burnt black as dirt
By the all-consuming passion of him
Who would take you like a hero. I am not he.
I am only he who sings this hymn

In praise of you and tells you truly he will come
And ravish you, destroy you,
Releasing you at last
That your progeny might live. I am no liar.
He will surely come. His name is Forest Fire.

Blowdown

The needles of this white pine
  Have turned from green to red,
As if a tree should be embarrassed
  For falling on its head.

It never stood especially tall
  But had a certain grace.
It crowned this little island
  And now has left a space.

I paddle round the granite slab
  To view the underside,
The root system that let the pine
  Shine and grow upright.

Here's the lowdown. Here's the dirt—
  Shocking, crude, and raw—
Roots like writhing snakes, like hands
  That, reaching, grasp and claw

To get those nutrients they need.
  They groped both night and day—
Thirsty, greedy from the seed—
  And still clutch clots of clay,

Lumps of loam, the bones of trees,
  Rocks the size of skulls.
To see these secrets of the soil
  Feels vaguely terrible.

A landmark's gone. I grieve it.
  The pine earned local fame,

A claim on our affection,
  And then the big wind came.

Those of us who pass this way
  Will feel that something's wrong,
Though hungry saplings pushing up
  Say: Not for long.

Solo

I woke from a dream about my first wife
To the tick-tick of leaves drifting down on the tent.
All these past lives! I saw stars
Spread like spawn in a still, black pond
And lay awake a long time, recalling old lovers,
Listening to wind strip leaves off the trees,
The cat-scream of one limb rubbing another.

The Otters

God knows, we would have been content with golden fish
That day, but the silver river overflowed with gifts.
As we held our glinting walleyes high to gloat and cheer,
A chuckling clan of otters suddenly appeared.
We hadn't seen their submarine approach. They just were there
And interested, exchanging our excited stares,
Submerging, bobbing up right close beside the boat
To gawk and peer. These living, breathing periscopes
Were talkative; they chattered, gurgled, hissed, and chirred
So that we whispered first, then laughed at what we heard.
Their playfulness and whiskers called up cats,
But the otters didn't mind their fur was running wet.
Some looked alert, concerned, but others just as glad
As children in some happy past that none of us had had.
Their beach ball buoyancy reminded us of seals.
Like seals, they seemed related, made us feel
As if these river silkies could easily turn human,
Slip their fur, emerge as little men and women.
Like us, they love their watersports. We saw them dive
To loop the loop, backfloat, flipflop, dunk, and rise.
Their posh pelts glistened, their pelage silver-gray
As the river and the rippling overcast that day
I saw that happiness was possible on earth,
At least in water, and what I witnessed gradually gave birth
To the dream that once upon a time we all were otters
And performed erotic undulations underwater.

Dead Gull

Did you fly too near the sun?
You look both burnt and drowned—
You, who transformed trash and stinking fish
To graceful flight, whose bones were light,
Whose cries were bright in the twinkling air.
You never wondered what you were
But coupled quickly with your kind,
Gobbled your food ecstatically,
Screamed at the world self-righteously,
Swooped and veered, climbed and hung
Splayed in the sky like a star. How far
You have fallen. The feathers of your carcass stir,
But you will not rise again. The autumn wind
Tears at my hair and makes a terrific noise.
God is a dog, and we are stuffed toys.

Chickadee

Like seedy stuff?
Can't get enough?
Ball of fluff
Seeks little puff.
Big appetite
But sleek and light.
Cute black cap
And black cravat,
White underthroat,
Gray overcoat.
Picks at bits
And likes to flit
Nice and quick
From stick to stick.
Would know your song
In any throng,
Those special notes
From your soft throat,
As sharp and sweet
As thistle seed.
Skills to weave
You won't believe.
Can build the nest
To your request.
Not too fussy.
Always busy.
Will not brood.
Will sing for food,
Go to and fro
At ten below.
Still will trill

When all is chill.
Downy soft
With lots of loft.
Like what you see?
Then check out me,
Chick chickadee,
Me, me, me, me,
Me, me, me, me!

Animals Glimpsed from the Road

Driving the high bridge over the bay,
I saw an eagle, real and regal,
Sailing at my side. Delighted,
Elated, for one full minute
I was a World War I fighter pilot
Steering my triplane through the wreckage
Of the heavens, cheered by my comrade, my chum,
Who protected my off-wing until he peeled away
And I descended to the distant, ordinary shore.

And then there was the wolf, my first,
For which I'd waited fifty years,
Listening with my skin, watching with my hair,
Whenever I ranged the woods,
Where I heard rumors, picked up scat.
But he showed up unpredictably,
Forty feet off the interstate, romping in the ditch,
An overgrown dog with heavy head,
Grizzled bronze and gold, gold-eyed,
And I was gone, whisked along in the traffic,
Pounding on the steering wheel and shouting,
"Wolf! A wolf! Son of a bitch!"

Not to mention that early summer moose,
Knee-deep in the bog at the bend of the road.
My brother hollered, "Whoa!"
And I obeyed, stopped cold,
Though we could have been hit from behind.
His coat was rough and scruffy,
Gunnysacks smeared with grease,
But he was a moose, all right, a mountain

Of flesh and fat, enough to feed a family
Well on through the winter. He looked
Rank and gamy, tough and dangerous,
Masculine to the core: wet beard, big prick,
A velvet crown of antlers he carried like a king.
What were we to make of such a living thing?

Or any of those many other sudden offerings?
The doe in her bright-red summer coat,
The raggedy vixen with her kit, dumb cluck
Spruce grouse, partridge off like a shot,
Scurry of squirrel, rabbity flash,
The great gray owl turning its face
Like a satellite dish, wink of weasel,
Slink of mink, the ass end of a bear?
Or that cougar I saw through veils of snow
Years ago on the Gunflint Trail,
The lash of its tawny tail.

We smashed through ancient kingdoms,
Ramming our wide highways home,
Rivers of concrete, tar, and gravel.
The animals had no choice. Nervous, edgy,
Exposed, they flushed along the margins.
Each creature, though, seemed a gift,
A luminescent moment that opened, froze the mind,
Before it melted. Always, I felt chilled, thrilled,
Washed and warmed with gladness, blessed.

But what did they mean to say,
Those animals glimpsed from the road? Nothing
Human at all? Or simply, "Hey!" "Hi!" "How do you do?"
I'd call these encounters accidents only,

Only darker thoughts are forming
In clouds at the back of my skull,
Thoughts that can't get through,
In a language I can't recall—shrieks,
Hoots, barks, growls, an agonizing howl—
Alarming, something sinister . . . a warning.

Black Bear Among Blueberries

for Dex Thue

At first he seemed a patch of dirt,
  But then we saw him move.
We paddled till our triceps hurt;
  He grew and slowly proved
A creeping bear, preoccupied
With fruit like fallen bits of sky.

My buddy's camera chirred and clicked.
  I steadied the canoe,
And then, to get a better look,
  He shouted, "Hey! Hey, you!"
The brute knew English well enough
To stand up straight and stare at us.

The bear looked like a patch of dirt
  In snaps the photo shop
Sent back. That burly, earthy spirit
  Had somehow slipped our trap.
The zoom had failed, or we had not
Been half as close as we had thought.

No evidence would help us brag
  About what we had seen,
His bulk and weight, his bristly shag
  So black it had a sheen,
Or how he rose, as tall as us,
To show that he could maul us.

He turned and ambled up the hill,
  Stepped through a wall of trees,

And though we knew they seldom kill
  Our kind, we walked uneasily
Across that hillside berry patch
And kept an eye out, naturally.

The place had been attacked, ransacked,
  Deadfalls overturned
For grubs, the boulders tilted back
  For beetles and sweet worms.
We crouched and filled our hats with fruit,
Though he had left few shrubs to loot.

Those berries taste like wind and sky.
  The hunger of that bear
Was not unlike our appetite,
  So why should we be scared?
It hardly seemed the jaws of death
Would exhale sweet blueberry breath.

And yet we eyed the ridgeline
  Where he had disappeared
Among the shadows of the jack pines
  And felt a twinge of fear.
This world was still a wilderness
Deserving awe and watchfulness.

Yellow Waterlilies on the Langley River

I slip and slither down the grassy riverbank,
Practically cartwheel and crash in the stream,
Recover and launch my peapod boat,
Slide beneath the small cement bridge,
And paddle black water for a short quarter mile,
Half dizzy, bedazzled by midsummer sun.

Now I turn, having seen more than enough
To know I'll be back on a lazier day.
The canoe comes about, and I hear myself shout,
"Where in the hell is Claude Monet?"

The bridge is gilded, the water glows,
Lilies lift their blossoms
Like small gold balls, the raised fists
Of infants rejoicing in heaven.
Rejoicing, I join them, Moses
In the bulrushes for fifteen minutes,
And Pharoah's men are far away.
If I waken, let me waken
To flowers and women.
The canoe is a coffin.
I'm crossing over.
Rock me. Rock me.
Rockabye, baby.

The lilies have leaves the size of saucers,
Scattered on the stream like green valentines.
I want to say, "I love you, too."
But there's nobody here
But black spruce, gold lilies,
The winking, blinking, glittering air.

Buddha's Fool

How will you get from here to there?
How on earth will you find the way?
Read the horizon. Look sharp. See
How the raggedy treeline sinks?
The portage is probably back in a bay.
Would you choose to hump over a hill
With packs or a boat on your back?
Look for the lows, a notch or a sag
That very well might be the place
Where a wiggling creek seeps in
Or lakewater leaks away.
With luck, you'll detect a blaze
Head-high on a shoreline tree,
A scar the size of your hand,
Where somebody long before you
Whacked off bark with an axe.
Say thanks. You've been given a sign,
A guide that could save your life
To lose on another day. Pull in
And watch out. This is a place
Where you might dump. Extract
The packs from the boat and rest
That fat one there in the shade.
The small one goes on your back.

Now you may flatten your palm
Against the smooth of the blaze.
This laying on of the hand
Reverses the faith healer's art,
For wood is good, as you know,
And energy flows up your arm.

You might want to freshen the wound,
Scraping it raw with a knife
To signal some other lost soul,
But likely you'd just as soon
The forest grew shut at your back.
So let it stay, silvery gray
As the sky on a cloudy day.

Now shoulder the narrow canoe
And vanish into the woods.
No telling what lies ahead—
You may wallow in goop to your thighs,
Bumble through boulders and stones,
Or creep up a slippery cliff.
If the trail is a comfortable rut,
You can put your faith in your feet
And those who have gone before,
But you've probably chosen a path
To take you out back of beyond,
Where you'll have to step over the dead
Trees in your way and big rocks
That call for hopscotch ballet.
You'll dance with the boat on your head
And just about now might recall
How the Buddha told us no man,
Having crossed the water to shore,
Would hoist the raft on his head
And bear it away overland.
Never mind. Have a laugh.
Say you went to a different school
Or confess that you're Buddha's fool.
At least if the sky drops rain,
You'll have a roof over your head.

But you can't live here. Push on.
If the path peters out at your feet,
Disappears in a heap of dry leaves,
You'll have to reverse, retreat
And search the trunks for a blaze,
A match for that sign on the shore,
To show you the way for sure.

Now, as you head uphill,
Still wearing your very large hat,
Your brow and chin both drip,
Your breath escapes in a hiss,
And you enter the world of myth.
You feel for your brother, Sisyphus,
And, reaching the ridgeline, revolt,
Easing the nose of the boat
Into the crotch of a birch,
And step out from under the weight.
Blood pumps into your neck;
The ache oozes out of your back.
You can breathe the peppermint air
And shake the bugs out of your hair.

You must take up your burden again,
Your arms upraised, outstretched,
As if you were falling headlong
Or shouting perpetual praise.
And now as you suffer uphill,
You utter the name of Christ.
You, too, have been scourged and lashed,
If only by branches and weeds.
You, too, have been torn by thorns,
But the blood that tickles your face

Has only been drawn by flies,
Who scribble their meaningless drivel
Inches before your eyes.
This dead-leg limping uphill
Is good for the heart but hard.
You can tell your body who's boss,
But every thirty-odd yards
The blazes slowly rise
Like stations of the cross.

You're glad for gravity now,
Pulling you thumping downhill,
Glad for that yellow swallowtail
Splayed on a balsam bough,
Glad for the magic of moss
And the deer mouse crossing the trail,
And though your breathing is wheezing now,
Your heart loud in your head,
Your mind stays cool and notices
Those blazes all are faces
Of the dead who rescued you:
That teacher who admonished you,
The uncle who took you to lunch,
That aunt who called you "dear" and "doll,"
Your dad, who ran beside your bike
And slowly let you go,
Your mother dreaming and smoothing the swell
Of her belly before you were born.

The dead go by in a blur,
And, gasping, faster, faster now,
You flash past the last blaze
And stumble on down to trail's end,

Teeter and rock, and now, dear God,
Push up, over, and drop
The impossibly heavy prow
In the buoyant blue water below.

You may feel you've finally arrived,
But once your hot head has cooled,
You'll remember, Buddha's fool,
You have to go back for that pack.
Walk, for the night is coming
Up over the edge of the earth,
And you shouldn't get caught in the dark,
Or you'll find yourself lost back there,
Embracing all the wrong trees,
Fingers groping rough bark,
Feeling for that smooth blaze
Like a blind man reading a face.

Stony River

I am trying to remember
That blue bend in the river,
The pines and yellow grasses.
How quickly my life passes.

The air out there was incense,
Essence of September.
Was it peppermint and anise?
I really can't remember.

I am trying to remember
The way the water glittered,
Sunlight like a benediction,
But that afternoon is gone.

I am trying to remember
Those minnows, bright as embers,
How like sparks they flashed and vanished
In the pool below the rapids.

I heard a bird or two, as I remember,
The splashing of my paddle in the river,
The trickle when I lifted it, and then there were
Those rumors in the breeze that made me shiver.

I am trying to remember
That eagle soaring over
And the shorebirds by the stones,
But those creatures all have flown.

Every autumn now I tell myself: Remember
To get out there on the river
Under golden leaves that cling to crooked branches.
We only get so many chances.

That daytrip through the jack pines and the willows
Is fading like the music of a cello.
Nothing in this life will last forever,
Though I hoped it might while floating down the river.

The Underword

As I knelt to clean the bass I'd caught,
I heard a sound a man might make
If he'd been slugged by a heavyweight,
The primitive expletive, "Unh!"
I grunted back, got a rude response,
So I walked to the lake to look.
A big bull moose stood across the way,
Up to his knees in the bay.
His hide looked smooth and shiny black;
His rack was fresh and huge.
He splashed along the distant shore,
Calling repeatedly, "Unh!"
What could he want? It couldn't be food.
There were lilies and sedges galore.
He was looking for love or a fight.
That groan recalled the guts of thought,
The sound beneath all speech,
A word from the land of Ur.
It was laden with pain, desire, and pride.
It said what I felt when my parents died,
When I first caught sight of my wife.
This was the poem I'd been waiting for,
True as the blade of a knife,
The original syllable, "Unh!"
I watched that bull march into the west,
Thrashing the silver water white,
Calling incessantly as he went,
As if he carried a wound.
Late September. The air grown cold.
I saw what the moose couldn't know:
As he waded into the dying light,
His antlers had turned to gold.

Pike Lake Lullaby

for Lilo

Clouds in the water,
Clouds in the sky.
Trees on the shoreline
Shine in the lake.
Am I dreaming I'm dreaming
Or finally awake?
My father is fading.
My mother is dirt.
I can't remember anything
About my birth.
So how did I get here?
I happened along.
The wind in the white pines
Sounds like a song
Saying, *Hush now. Quiet.*
Nothing is wrong.

from

The Reindeer Camps
and Other Poems

(2012)

Nestlings

The blue smoke stank, the chainsaws snarled,
The popples thrashed and thumped the ground.
Of all my memories of that world,
Why should this keep coming round?

I stood way back—excited, sad—
As light exploded through the shade.
The swarming men all knew my dad,
Which made me somewhat less afraid.

But then big Nils called out to me,
And I walked over, hesitant,
Where he had limbed a fallen tree.
"Look," he said, and crooked a hand.

The wood gave off a pungent scent.
Sawdust powdered Nils' wrists.
Hands on knees, I slowly bent
To see where he said, "Look at this."

The pale green trunk, smooth as skin,
Was punctured by a perfect hole;
Woodpecker nestlings peeped within,
Featherless and vulnerable.

I smiled at Nils. He grinned at me
And placed a huge hand on my head.
"We'll tie this to another tree
So the parent birds come back," he said.

I don't remember that they did.
Undoubtedly, those nestlings died.
The frightened parents must have fled,
But I like thinking how Nils tried.

That site where our new house was built
Got cleared of scrapwood in one day,
But I was touched by fear and guilt,
A shadow that would stay.

The Pit

The abandoned pit was our Wild West,
    Where we galloped on foot and then
Lit up our stolen cigarettes,
    Midget Marlboro men.

This Western landscape came complete
    With an aspen grove and ponds.
The willows grew where we soaked our feet
    And dozed in soft green fronds.

There were buttes and canyons in this world
    The gravel men had left,
Where we watched the swallows sail and swirl.
    They nested in the cliffs.

We dared to stare in badger holes,
    To sample the abyss,
Preparing for our grown-up roles,
    For deeper darknesses.

Of all our days at the gravel pit,
    There's one that haunts me most,
When each boy clambered up a butte
    To strip off all his clothes.

These pedestals weren't far apart;
    We could shout to one another.
But I felt alone with my thudding heart,
    Like Isaac on his altar.

The breeze blew softly over me;
  The light was woman-warm.
I was cradled by some mystery
  And watched myself grow hard.

I've never fully understood:
  Was it sex? Was it religion?
Each boy lay bare on a grassy butte,
  Defenseless under heaven.

Dead Evergreens

These trees along the shoreline,
  Veiled in pale green gauze,
Remind me of old women
  Who simply won't be bossed

To lie down in the nursing home
  Or quit their cigarettes.
They stay up late with paperbacks
  And seldom call their kids.

Their kids can argue till they're hoarse
  And purple in the face.
They never cared that much for town.
  They've sunk roots in this place.

And here's that bearded hermit,
  Who let his hair go wild,
Whose clothes hung loose as birch bark,
  Though he flashed a gentle smile.

He came to town four times a year
  To meet his few desires.
He did his own damn dentistry
  With whiskey and a pliers.

They say he lived on venison,
  Pickled fish, and berries,
That birds would flutter to his hand,
  Though children thought him scary.

This hunched and twisted cedar
   Looks like a man I knew
Who had to crawl from room to room.
   His dog was crippled, too.

He stuck like lichen to his farm
   And milked a dozen cows
Till a corporate decision
   Finally shut him down.

He'd fry a pan of pork chops
   And cut big chunks of cake.
"Eat up!" he'd shout. "There's one thing
   That nobody can take."

These trees are clearly done for,
   Bound to drop and drown,
But, silver-gray and sturdy still,
   They somehow hold their ground.

I've cut them, feeling desperate,
   Shivering for heat.
Their limbs flashed incandescent.
   Their scent was smoky sweet.

Several Dozen Shades of Green

Down here in the ravine, we have the model
By means of which the sad United Nations
Might actually succeed: Every species
Flies its own peculiar flag—
Raggedy valerian, broadleaf maple, pom-pom of the pine,
The ferns unfurled, tassels of the grass,
And the willow drags its drooping pennants in the water.
Each declares, defiantly, its own identity,
All compete for space and spread and height,
And yet they've all agreed somehow
To work together for the greater good of green.
And aren't we lucky things turned out this way?
What if leaves had been taxicab yellow or, worse yet,
        dull as mud?
Think how jumpy we'd have been or seriously depressed!
Instead, we are soothed and encouraged by green, made
        semi-serene,
At least for a season, though those of us who walk here
        in December know
This great glorification of chlorophyll, these snowflakes
        formed of cellulose,
This crisscross reach and rush of vegetation
        is just a passing dream.

The Minnesota Department of Transportation Plans to Straighten Out Highway 1

Was the Department of Transportation
Created to break our starved hearts?
So it would seem. They bulldoze dreams.
Once, where we blasted across a high bridge
And glimpsed, through a lattice of steel,
The flash of the black-and-blue river,
A raft of bluebills aswim in a swirl,
The thrashing white rapids below,
Our looks now boomerang off a blank wall,
The highway turned hallway, one more
Aesthetic atrocity committed, one more
Beauty spot blotted out.

And now they intend to tame Highway 1,
That sweet prime number, that first and best
Rambunctious trunk through the trees,
That primitive, asphalt snake in the woods,
That whoop-de-doo carnival ride of a road.
Oh, say it ain't so! Oh, no, no, no.
Didn't these planners have fathers at all
To tell them the journey itself is the goal?
Were their poor mothers so hooked on speed
They could only whisper, *"Efficiency!"*?
Oh, say it ain't so. Oh, no.

Will we allow them to level the lift
And fall, the swoop and drop,
The rockabye-baby ocean motion
Singing through our spinning wheels,

The lilt of the lullaby lay of the land?
No, no. No more tilt-a-whirl, watch out,
Hit the gas, touch the brake, wake up,
Hug the curve, sliding, gliding, off on a bowbend,
Double back, hairpin, stop-and-go waltz?
Will all this be lost? To what end, pray tell.
To arrive more quickly at a gravel pit
Or the big blue nothing of Lake Superior?

Whoa, Nelly. Don't tell me
We should speed past trees that took
Two hundred years and more to be
The colossal candelabras they've finally become.
Says who? Should MNDOT reduce
Our chance to flush a flustered grouse,
Waken a wolf, startle a deer, frighten a fox,
Or collide with the sudden broad side of a moose?

Save us, preserve us from Euclid's dream,
The gleam in the architect's eye. Leave us
This road like a river's meander through popple and pine.
Let planners surrender their pens, resign.

Mink

The mink is a slinky, sly critter
   But quick as a fart when he wants
To dash through his crosshatched habitat
   Of riverine forest and swamp

To straighten a snake from its wiggle,
   Nab a rabbit who's strayed from its house
And bite at the neck until dead,
   Or crunch a warm mouthful of mouse.

He rejects the gossip of red squirrels
   And steers clear of otters, the clowns.
This overgrown weasel's a loner
   Who'll mate but won't hang around.

Except for some white at the collar,
   His coat is dark chocolate brown.
He moves like a shadow in shadows
   And loves to play lost and found.

Camped once on a hump of black gabbro,
   My brother and I caught five pike
And piled their entrails nearby,
   Thinking gulls would clean up the site.

But a mink emerged from the fractures
   That shattered that long point of rock,
Made an undulant run for the gutpile,
   And then we heard mink happytalk.

He dragged the remains of each northern
    To his cleft in the rocks down below,
Which magnified growls, urgent slurping,
    And chuckles I'd translate like so:

Oh, chewy, salt goo of intestine!
    Oh, tender fish liver and heart!
Oh, succulent, sweet juice of eyeball!
    Oh, which is my favorite part?

So, wealthy women of fashion
    And overpaid athletes, take note
Of the greedy-guts eater you've chosen
    To serve as your totem and robe.

River Otter Rag

Sweetwater seal,
Hide-and-go-seeker,
Slippery slider,
Smooth water glider,
You bob and go under,
Awakening wonder.

How can you swim
So far, so long
Where light grows dim
And there's no oxygen?
Did you learn this trick when you were young,
Or were you born with an extra lung?

Were you once a badger
But such a mud lover
That, thrashing through bushes,
You slid among rushes,
Dissolving in water
To surface as otter?

Hissyfit spitter,
Sneezer and wheezer,
Snuffling blowhard,
Why is your chatter
And spluttering blather
So humanly pleasing?

Cruncher of crayfish,
Ingester of insects,
Robber of birds' nests,

You swallow the walleye,
Smelting the bones
In your Bessemer belly.

Ice and snow skidder,
Prankster and kidder,
You dolphin the river
With siblings in summer,
Your brash bravura a
Buoyant brouhaha.

Does play have a purpose?
Amphibious porpoise,
What is your lesson?
That families are fun
And it's ducky to dive?
That we're plumb lucky to be alive?

Unsinkable soap,
Peekaboo periscope,
Curious creature,
Exemplary teacher,
What is it you see
When you gawk back at me?

An Afterlife After All

After our dog survived to fifteen or a hundred and five,
After she'd shrugged out of every harness and collar
     we could devise,
After we'd fenced her and yet she ran but always returned,
     laughing, teaching us dogs could laugh,
After hauling small children on sleds and yanking
     her leash till she coughed,
After tearing the stuffing from Stumpy and Stocky
     and other stuffed toys,
After the fetching of sticks, which she kept to herself,
After wearing the chinchilla's cage, including chinchilla,
     like an outsized, hysterical hat,
After stashing strange gifts of dry bread in our neatly made
     beds,
After the kidnap, driven two hundred miles by people
     convinced that she was their dead pet come back,
After the rescue and her triumphant return,
After teaching us "walk" was a dangerous word that could
     whip her into a whining canine whirligig,
After thousands of rambles along Chester Creek, with
     sniffing, bushwhacking, and belly-deep wading of pools
     for the cool and the lapping of sweet, wild water,
After her muzzle went white and she gradually slowed,
She lost a tooth, and we sat beside her for hours,
     watching her bleed and drool.

After my wife brought her home from the vet, eyes wet,
Having heard the man say "mandibular cancer" and
     "moving fast,"
We kept her three days, and after she stood at her dish
     and just looked at us,

We knew what we had to do. We dug out her grave
By shovel and pick and by hand, inching through rocks,
    roots, and clay
And walked her three times that last day
And, brushing and brushing, burnished her fur till she shone,
And she received compliments on her looks on the very
last day of her life.

After boosting her into the back of the car,
After waiting long minutes inside a bare room,
After she sank to the floor and cooled her belly on tile,
The veterinarian entered and stood with his arms at his sides
And kept saying "mercy" like some sort of priest,
And after the laying of hands on her body,
She winced as the needle entered, then slowly relaxed
And lowered her eyelids and lowered her head,
And once her great heart could no longer be heard,
We loaded her into the back of the car and drove home.

After we carried her heavily to the hole,
After we laid a white sheet smooth in the red clay pit,
After uncinching her collar with jingling tags,
After we draped her warm, slack body into the grave,
Her blonde and mahogany fur fit for a Viking queen,
After we placed sweet basswood blooms at her throat,
Then shut her from sight for good with the sheet,
After we raked the dirt over her crumbly and smooth,
And, after some days, found a heart-shaped rock for
    her headstone
And planted hostas to cover the naked place where she lay,
I finally went for a walk, free of this creature at last.

Free to wander wherever, however long I might wish,
I wished to walk once more the green ravine she had loved,
Free of dog duty at last, no longer trailing that mutt,
But found, as she'd beat me around every bend,
Then returned to check on my progress, that she was
        already there,
Everywhere, after preceding me into the Valley of Death,
Gazing back for a moment from every bend in the path,
As if to say, "Are you coming?"

After years of disbelieving in heaven
And laughing off any Valhalla for pets,
I saw that, after all, there was this afterlife at least,
Our living, diminishing memories of the dead,
And I said, through my disbelief and the fog of my grief,
To the ghost of this very old girl in my head,
"Good dog, dead dog, good dog."

The Pileated Woodpecker

Is black and jumbo, like a crow.
Whenever I spot one, I go, "Oh!"
Among the birds I like the best,
He has a shocking scarlet crest
And looks terrific in the snow.
He's got a lightning streak of white
From beak to neck and down his side.
There's white beneath his inky wings,
And when he flies, it's startling.
His call goes *whicker, whicker, whicker,*
Not unlike—though louder than—the smaller flicker.
You'll see him swoop from trunk to trunk
And hammer holes that who'd have thunk
A bird could make with head and bill,
But he's the one responsible.
He's after grubs, a heavy feeder,
Much like me, a big meat-eater.
He loves the fragrant northern forest,
And I do, too, of course,
So it's possible that we're related,
Me and the pileated.

Nightnoise

Ducks talk quietly among the barren stalks,
Quarreling incessantly. Who should lead the flock?

Muskrat bloops below the surface of the stream.
Moon covers everything with light like cream.

Back in the forest, did a branch go screak?
Last of the mosquitoes wants to bite my cheek.

Mice like to rummage in the pots and pans.
Beaver whacks the water like a screen-door slam.

Starlight crackles in the cold night air.
Nothing makes a noise, and it isn't even there.

With You in Spain

Even though you'd gone to Spain,
The tulips came
Up like bright umbrellas yanked
Open by the wind
So that I grinned
And gave small thanks,
Even though you'd gone to Spain.

The lilacs held their soft
Sprays of lavender aloft
And made me glad,
Though I was sad
Because you'd gone to Spain.

My inner life was drab
Without you, but the flowering crab
Effervesced like pink
Champagne, a soft shellburst
Of fireworks
At which I blinked.
To think that such a color
Could occur
With you in Spain!

The apple by the garden
Bore big blooms like white gardenias,
Ghostly glimmerings of moonlight
That glistered in the night,
But you missed your chance to see this
Because you'd gone to Spain.

The waves of blue forget-me-nots
That broke about the house were not
Meant for my eyes only,
So I absorbed their lowly
Beauty for us both, hoping you were homesick
For this side of the Atlantic
There in Spain.

Oh, I knew that you'd come back
And we'd glory in the crack
As you told stories
Both laughable and scary
And taught me Spanish names
For blossoms, trees, and rain.
My heart was hardly broken
Just because we hadn't spoken
Face-to-face for weeks.
That muscle's strong and sleek,
But it *was* severely strained
With you in Spain.

My nerves were somewhat numb,
But I could smell and see
The tiny blossoms of the plum
Invite the thirsty bees,
And I was pleased
To watch them come,
Though they were dumb
About your whereabouts
In Spain.

I doubt
I can explain

The half of what you missed
By going off to Spain,
But if a tree blooms in the forest
And there's no one there to notice,
Is that lonesome festival of beauty real?
And how can unseen flowers hold appeal
For you in Spain?

I confess I walked the orchard,
Indulging in self-torture,
Envisioned us erased,
Another couple in our place,
Who seldom gave a thought
To those who'd planted what they'd bought.
The apples, plums, and cherries
Still remained and could be seen
In sunshine and in rain
But not by you and me.
Though the thought was little help,
I tried to tell myself
When we are dead and buried
It will only be
As if we'd gone to Spain.

Let me try to make this plain.
Imagine you had seen
Apple petals drifting down
Like manna on the lawn,
But we were gone.

from The Reindeer Camps

4.

Two kinds of reindeer in this world:
Wild and half tame. Here is how
Reindeer came to live with us.
We hunted them, we followed them.
Dozens, hundreds, thousands
Flowed across the land like living lava.
Compared to them, we were so few
They did not panic at our camps.

One day one woman noticed
Females eating reindeer moss
Where she had pissed. They liked the salt.
So every day she urinated closer to her tent
Until, at last, they came, oh, yes,
Close enough to touch. She touched.
They let her pet, caress, and milk them.
So they came to live with us.
And wasn't that a crafty trade that woman made—
Milk and meat and bone and fur
For nothing more than urine?

7.

We walk and ride from camp to camp,
From spring to autumn slaughter,
From snow to rain and bugs to snow,
And seldom settle anywhere
For longer than a month or so.
To overgraze the grass and moss
Would be a grave mistake.

At dawn the deer disperse to feed
Through valley, mountain, wood.
We follow, keeping watch, with dogs,
And nudge them home at dusk.
We spook them just enough so that
They cluster, counterclockwise,
Turn and turn and tighten
In a breathing knot for night.

There may be berries in the woods,
A fragrant grove of larch,
A sweet supply of fish nearby;
That can't be helped. We move
To guard the grass and moss,
Which means to save the deer,
In other words, ourselves. We move,
And when we do, we don't look back.
We never say goodbye.
To say so sadly might imply
That someone's going to die.
But we are people of the deer,
And we come back by going on,
Appearing here next year.

8.

Lucky the man whose love loves him
And also loves the reindeer camps.
Women like the village now,
To work as teacher, nurse, or clerk,
To walk the street in long cloth coats,
To wear the shiny leather boots,
Pretending they're in Moscow.
The herders who come into town

Seem strange to them, can't talk
From listening closely to the wind,
To wolves, to grunting beasts whose hooves
Clatter over stone like clicking castanets.
Lucky the boy who finds a girl
Who loves the rippling willow leaves
Like minnows in the blue,
Who loves the shine of poplar leaves,
Their shifting in the sun,
Who loves the scent of larch needles,
Their perfume in the tent,
Who doesn't mind the rain and damp
But loves the ways to warm.
Lucky the man whose love loves him
But also loves the reindeer camps.

11.
Taiga, taiga, world of white,
Home to sable, black as night,
What mere human mind or eye
Can take in your immensity?

In which valley, deep with snow,
Does the reindeer lichen grow?
Will a white owl lead the way?
Broken voiced, can raven say?

Who might know in this domain?
Brown bear? Marten? Wolverine?
Since we've lost the shaman's drum,
Where will second sight come from?

Who will wear the antler crown,
Dance until he's fallen down,

Go inside to travel far,
Find out where best pastures are?

In this land of little sticks,
Who will heal the mad and sick,
Show the drumskin smeared with gore
After health has been restored?

Taiga, taiga, world gone white,
Home to sable, black as night,
What mere human mind or eye
Can penetrate your mystery?

14.
How long have we herded reindeer?
Three thousand years.
How long have we hunted reindeer?
Ten thousand years.
How come, having died, then,
You're still surprised to see
Your favorite turn to gaze at you
Through frosty breath? As you
Approach, he walks away, then trots
As you begin to run,
And only as you sprint flat out
And sob for breath and flail,
You catch one antler at the root
Like someone clutching at
A sapling trunk while falling from a cliff.
You pull yourself at last
Upon his muscled, rippling back
And clutch both antlers now
Because he's running lightfoot free

And lifting off the ground,
So fast the tears flow from your eyes,
But still you see you're flying,
Flying toward the sun, the life
Beyond your life at last,
Finally begun.

from

Chester Creek Ravine

(2015)

A stem of lupine
Left on the sign
For the hiking trail.

Thunder of the creek!
With so much noise, who can hear
The song sparrow speak?

In sneakers and a stocking cap,
The pregnant girl throws a stick,
And there goes her black lab!

Winter, slow to go,
Went north, then came back overnight.
Robins in the snow.

Branches, even logs,
Wash past in fast water.
"Hey!" I call the dog.

Who wants to be responsible?
Why not sit out all night? The glint
Of a bum's pint bottle.

Our beautiful friend
Is dying of cancer; the buds
Keep coming anyway.

How the dog's tail wags!
I bring home wildflowers
And windblown plastic bags.

In streamside scenery,
The best part is invisible:
Birdsong in the greenery.

At last let out of school,
The boy with thick-lensed glasses
Stands knee-deep in the pool.

I thought I was alone,
But I hear women's voices,
Water over stone.

Chin-deep in clover,
The chipmunk quits chewing
To look me over.

Dan, the volunteer,
Repairs the path with mud. He,
Too, is thoroughly smeared.

Carrying his kill,
The goshawk cut across the path.
I hear wingbeats still.

Riding in a chestpack,
Babbling nonsense, the baby
Makes her mother laugh.

A robin hurries past.
A few yellow willow leaves
Have fallen in the path.

Water flies right off the cliff.
Too late to say,
"Wait now. What if . . ."

No one scattered these
Golden popple leaves, yet we
Proceed like royalty.

Here's a water bead
On a tiny moccasin
Of the jewelweed.

Now, as she grows older,
She often stops to lay a hand
On this mossy boulder.

White-throated sparrows,
With their pine-scented songs,
Will be gone tomorrow.

A bad election
Last night. Below the bridge
At dawn: smashed pumpkins.

The wind gave the trees
Such a thrashing I felt
Sorry for the bees.

Where have all the hikers gone?
The fire ring beside the stream
Filled with fallen leaves.

Now their seeds are shed,
Pale grasses wait
With clasped hands and bowed heads.

Summer's truly gone.
Creek ice forms overnight;
Light snow falls at dawn.

I've got my share of woe;
The mountain ash berries
Carry loads of snow.

The dog acts finicky
As she surveys first ice this year . . .
Then crosses quickly, quickly!

Out here in the cold,
The woodpeckers tap telegraph,
But we can't crack their code.

In colored coveralls,
The climbers talk a long time
Below the frozen falls.

Everything shrunk tight.
The sun hangs in the sky,
An Inuit drum.

Winter's fierce and long,
But isn't that the chickadee's
Two-note mating song?

from

Nordic Accordion
Poems in a Scandinavian Mood

(2018)

Tussocks

Right here on the edge
Of memory and everything
That matters most,
My father leads me from
His father's house, where
Old people speak Swedish
I can't understand, and
Here we go, in gloves and woolen jackets,
Up the hill and slanting down
Across the stubble hayfield
Into trees and through
The spooky woods, emerging
At the marsh. Ducks
Explode from yellow grass
And startle me. They fly away,
And everything grows quiet
Once again, more silent
Than before. *Quack.*
Quiet, quiet, quiet—*quack*,
A fading sound, far off.

And now my father says
We're going to cross the marsh.
But how? There's water,
Splinterings of ice.
He points out
Bumpy lumps of grass,
Like little islands.
These are tussocks.
You jump from hump
To hump, and so

We hopscotch
Cross the marsh,
Frightening and fun.
Towards the end,
I slip. Icy water
Sucks my foot.
My father grabs my hand
And swings me to the land.

We climb a grassy rise
And stretch out, warmed
By morning sun, bare branches
High above. He tells me
How he came here as a boy
With brothers, who are uncles
Now that *I'm* the boy,
And one of them is dead (the war),
To watch the wildlife below.
And there! A flock of wood ducks,
Extravagantly colored, coast
Back home and curl the water as they land.
Years from now, I'll find
His penny notebook with the drawings—
Duck and mink and rabbit—
And excited scribbling, drifting smoke
Of how the turning seasons
Burned with meaning then.

I don't know too much
This morning on the hillside
Since I'm only four or five.
It will be half a century
Before I learn third-hand

That just a few years earlier
My father woke to find his friend
In the foxhole next to his
Hacked to pieces in the night,
Reported that attack, then joined—
This peaceable and loving man—
His captain's group
Of volunteers who hunted
Down that Japanese patrol
And killed them, every one.

The world is full of dangers,
But I'm ignorant this morning,
And we've crossed the swampy spot
On tussocks, as I'll cross the world
Throughout my days, remembering,
Deep down, beneath awareness,
How to find this sunshot hillside
Where a faint perfume of woodsmoke
Drifts like incense on the wind
And my father snugs me to his side.

A Taste for Ptarmigan

On December first, it snowed a foot.
On the second, it snowed two more. Then
It quit and turned off cold, so
Cars refused to start and people just sat still.
Musk ox weather, day by day.
The nights were spooky, too. Boom!
You'd hear the ice crack on the lake
Or, worse, the rafters in your house.
Nails popped. The screws came loose.
You still had windows, but what could you see
With frost flowers grown fantastically opaque?

New Year's Day, it snowed an inch.
On the second, we got two. On the third,
Three inches more. I said to the wife,
"What's the use?" She passed the sugar bowl.
I sprinkled some over my flakes, repulsed because
The crystals fell like you-know-what, but
I needed the oomph to shovel the roof.
I got right down to shingles. That night, a blizzard hit.
Everywhere I looked looked white. Salt. Sheets.
The tablecloth. The fish in my *mojakka*.

Open the door, you'd close it quick: snowy owls
On the rooftops. Snow leopards in the streets.
Crows had fled the country, replaced by ptarmigan.
I grabbed the .410 and blasted one.
The oven still worked, so we seasoned the bird,
And I'll say this: It wasn't bad. Not bad at all.
Tasted a little like chicken, with a hint of juniper.

Our hair was turning white. The wife was
Fading, pale, her brown eyes going gray.
One morning, gazing down on her in bed,
I thought she looked so pitiful and snug,
I said, "You might as well stay in your drift."
I brewed her a cup of tea but didn't add any cream.
I brought it to her nice and hot . . . and black
As garden earth we turn up in the spring.
She reached out a ghostly hand and said,
"Baby, come on inside."

She treated me so sweet that I saw fireworks
And lost all track of time. When I woke up,
The robins sang, and kids were playing catch.
Neighbors came to lunch on the lawn.
The wife was toasty brown. By nightfall, though,
I longed for a hockey game, and, leafing through
The calendar, I daydreamed flakes and drifts
And felt a strange affection for the ice cubes in my drink.

Cotton Grass

About the time trout start to bite, you might
Be driving the back roads or out for a hike
And stop at the sight of . . . what? . . .
Receding snow? Surveyor's flags?
Dozens of daisies? No. Fluffed by the breeze,
Cotton grass brightens the greening meadow
Edging the black spruce bog.

It's a sedge, not grass, but does not care
What you call it—ghost grass, wool grass,
White delight, dauber-on-stiff-stem,
Jittery-joy-of-this-June-day—
As a killdeer cries nearby.

Its root stalks like wet ground,
So the little white flags signal Danger.
Bog Warning. Back Off. Stay Clear.
Or you might get sucked out of sight
And turn to tar, sunk in ick-black peat.

What should you make of this
Modest beauty that circles the globe,
Contiguous with hardy tribes
Of the Circumpolar Bear Cult?
The fibers of cotton grass heads are too brittle
To spin into thread, but Swedes
Have stuffed pillows with ghost grass.
Imagine. Imagine their dreams.

Up in the Land of Dwarf Willow,
The Yupik have twisted them into candlewicks,

The Finns have used them as tinder,
Which takes the spark, which grows to flame,
The red wolf that drives off the dark.
Scots found wool grass will dress wounds.
Siberians swear that chewing the stem
Will dry up your diarrhea.

These knee-high plant people stand their damp ground.
Their white flags flutter in place, so you think
They are stuck in the mud, but
They do move. Even now, right here,
As you watch, their anthem, the wind, is rising.
Their tufted seeds loosen and lift aloft
To ride the skies, and then, thanks
To their silken parachutes, softly, softly
Descend. Cotton grass circles the globe.

How They Handled Alva's Calf

Alva had the cutest calf
She treated like a special pet.
A cowgirl shouldn't act like that,
But she was just a calf, herself.

Then Sanna fell and broke her leg.
We knew we'd have to slaughter her.
"Waste not, want not" was our motto.
Sobbing, Alva wailed and begged

Me and Solvig if we'd butcher,
She would herd our cows all day.
We took pity, whet our knives,
Killing time till we could watch her

Lead the cattle out of sight.
Solvig drew back Sanna's head.
I cut clean across her throat.
We'd seen this often, did it right.

To make a pudding that we liked,
We placed a pan to catch the blood,
Then strung her up and peeled the hide,
So small it was pathetic.

The jays knew it was time to eat.
Several gathered in the trees,
And they came swooping down
When Solvig held out bits of meat.

We had a fire smoking hot,
And, hungry from the bloody work,
We spit some chunks on alder sticks
To roast, then ate them on the spot.

My, but she was tender! Veal,
I guess a butcher might have said.
She'd made an entertaining pet
But made an even better meal.

Her guts were piled on the ground.
We'd clean her small intestines, too,
But still had lots of meat to dress—
Big job, but no one else around.

Elbow-deep in all this mess,
Our faces sweaty, dark with soot,
We heard this fellow shout, "Hello?"
A man who'd brought supplies to us.

Our arms were smeared with blood and fat.
The shock that showed on that man's face!
He must have wondered what on earth
It was that he was looking at!

Hedda Left Behind

There was this old woman, Hedda,
   Annalisa's mother's aunt,
   Who treated all us girls like friends,
Though she loved nature more than people.

Working at the cow camp every year
   For many summers—sixty odd—
   Hedda lost her faith in God.
She believed in trees and pasture.

Hedda had a way with cows and goats,
   As if she spoke their language.
   That woman could engage
The smallest birds by whistling their notes.

Talking with you, she'd forget
   Herself and moo, maybe, or growl,
   Or hoot a little, like an owl.
Today, they'd say she had Tourette's.

To us, she just was old Aunt Hedda.
   Hedda smoked a pipe. She told stories.
   Some were sweet, but I preferred them gory.
I can't forget Aunt Hedda, ever.

Once she fell, she came out crooked,
   Yet she still limped up to camp,
   Where she could trim and shine the lamps
And do a little cooking.

Finally she grew so weak
   She simply could not make the trip.
   I heard her family's men drew slips
To choose who'd have to speak.

That year, she stood out in her yard
   To watch us go, holding to a tree.
   I never dreamed I'd have to see
An old one cry so hard.

Runes of the North

Birch bark starts. Cedar's fast.
Ash and maple last.

Quick say-so
May not know.

Even those on skis must pee.

Rooms in big houses often stand empty.
Two words to study. They are "good plenty."

Polka, two-step, schottische, waltz.
She won't be impressed by somersaults.

Off-lake winds are wild.
Off-shore leaves a lonely child.

If you've got your big fat head attached,
You won't wear snowshoes to a boxing match.

A simple life has grace. Endure. Observe
The smooth axe handle's curve.

An oar is not a paddle.
The horse goes underneath the saddle.

Thorfinn, Thorkel, and Snorri was here.

Worried looks are allowed.
Even the bear keeps an eye out.

Those people aren't singing.
They're Swedish.

Crows are smarter than you think.
Don't think those birds don't think.

Got himself a snow machine
But wouldn't know a wolf from a wolverine.

In a pinch, an igloo will do
But probably not for you.

An Evening of Swedish Folk Songs

There are bony brown cows in this music,
Mugs of hot milk spiced with pepper.
The last few asters of autumn are here,
The first flickering flakes of snow.
Moonlight is trapped in these tunes,
The cries of white-haired women,
And the wind sneaks in beneath the door.
Here is the breadknife my sister stuck
     in the landlord's guts,
A Bible, a candle, and a birchbark bowl
In the low-slung hut made of sod and sticks
Where I lived six hundred years ago.

from

So Surprised to Find You Here

(2022)

Marsh Marigolds

The hiking trail takes me uphill
And then through wetlands in the woods,
The river still ahead. It's dark
In here, the water black. I slosh
Through shallow pools, rock hop,
Cross a crude boardwalk, and notice
Marigolds, marsh marigolds,
Half grown but glowing in the dusk,
Their cup-shaped, deep green leaves
Still small, their yellow flowers
Still more bud than bloom, and think
Of country girls with whom I went
To grade school way back when.
Jeanie, Sandy, Margie, Joyce . . .
I'm so surprised to find you here,
Half hidden in the cedar shade,
And after all these years.

Three Big Rocks

1.

I'm no geologist,
But I do like a good-sized rock.
Fishing the Cloquet the other day,
Catching nothing but snags,
I followed a trail other feet had worn
In the grass along the riverbank,
Casting as I went. A nasty business.
The river was chockfull of rocks,
So I kept on till the faint path petered out,
Beyond where I had ever been.
The bank was bouldery now,
Black rocks big as dinosaur eggs.
When the going grew too scary,
I girded my loins, as the Bible
Seems to recommend,
Plunged off in the woods,
And fought the thorny brush.

Bless me, breaking through,
I found the water smooth, and,
At the river's edge, a rock
The size of a compact car.

Clambering onto this platform,
I stood, though it slanted riverward,
And, casting out midstream, struck
A hole two boxcars long, where,
If I could drop my bait in there,
A heavy pull came every couple casts
And a consequent tussle with thrashing

And hauling and sometimes a leap and a splash.
Over two hours, I pulled in sixteen
Fish: golden walleyes, emerald pike,
The pewter of rock bass,
Smallmouth in their scales of bronze.

I kept the largest and let the rest go.
This was a location to remember, so I christened
My discovery on the spot, pronouncing it
    The Big Rock.

    2.
The first time I saw Sweden,
My cousin showed my wife and me
Broad blue rushing rivers,
The lake where church boats race,
The cabins of my ancestors,
The church where, once upon a time,
My great-grandfather led the hymns
With a one-string instrument.
She pointed out the pasture camps
Hidden in the hills, where women herded cows
For centuries, their wild songs drifting down the slopes.
And down we went, in slickers and hard hats,
In the famous Falun copper mine.
We got an eyeful, that's for sure, but
Driving back from one of our forays,
She grinned and said, "Let's have a look at this."

The sign read, *"Stora Sten."*
Sten, we knew, meant rock or stone,
But *stor* could mean a dozen things:
Distinguished, great, funny, wide,

Delightful, lovely, big . . . My cousin
Would not translate, but led us on
A path into the dusky woods,
Which darkened as we walked
The winding trail through spruce trees
Crowding close. But then there came
A kind of opening, and there it loomed:
The *Stora Sten,* a rough gray block of granite
Five times taller than we stood,
The size of a chapel, say, although
It had no windows. What a thing to see
Out here in all these trees, surrounding it
Like soldiers in dark uniforms. It looked
Like something you could pray to,
Your forehead pressed against its mossy side,
And so we gave it several minutes of respect.
Yet it was just absurd, some kind of
Joke the gods had dropped out of the sky.
We gazed, then met each other's eyes,
Exploding into laughter,
Although we did not speak
As we felt our way back to the car.
On our way home, our talk kept flashing
With two words that signified the mystery
We'd witnessed: *stora sten*—great big rock,
Lovely rock, delightful rock, distinguished rock—
    Stora Sten.

    3.
Up along the Manitoba border,
Where the land lies flat as slate,
The fields grow green with hay,
Cerulean with flax, glorious

With sunflowers. Yet
Winter's never far away.
Blizzards blast that place.

The wide sky is pierced by the spire
Of Pine Creek Lutheran Church,
Like a rocket on its launching pad.
I was raised here, and that steeple
Always moves me as it lifts,
A sword against the sky.

Reading in the memory book
Of that dwindling congregation,
I was struck by a woman who,
Though she loved that isolated church,
Declared her fondest recollections
Involved those times the parish met
At The Big Stone in the clearing
In the jack pines by The Bog.
I, myself, was never there,
But I can see it. I've seen photos:
Pale gray granite, ten feet high,
Its edges rounded off, about
The size of a pickup truck.

I know just enough geology
To understand such rocks are called
Erratics, having been transported
So far from their origins
Upon the backs of glaciers
And left lying, willy-nilly,
On such plains as this one,
Where the prairie meets the pines.

And I know humans just enough
To understand we're drawn to them,
Though not exactly why.

These people were erratics, too,
Carried far from Iceland, Norway,
Sweden, Denmark, with names
Like Lislegaard and Nordvall,
Dropping here, as they will say,
"Way up north of nowhere."

Gazing at their old snapshots,
My mind makes movies, and in this one,
They've already held a service
Where the pastor offered up a prayer,
Giving thanks for this fine day.
They've sung some favorite hymns—
"Rock of Ages," maybe, or
"The Church's One Foundation."
Now, though, they sing,
"Be present at our table, Lord,"
Although there is no table, but there is
This one gigantic rock, from which
No one will stray too far.

The women, wearing dresses,
Naturally, and quite a few in hats,
Display the offerings they've brought—
Chicken, hot dish, salads, pie—
And call the children off the summit of the stone.
The men, in darker clothes, cloth caps, fedoras,
Lean against the rock, and several smoke.
These people all are sinners, and they know it.

Helga envies Jennie's looks, and Arvid wouldn't mind
Helping Severt lose a tooth or two some Saturday in town,
But this is Sunday, they are neighbors, so they get along,
Gathered round this lodestone which attracted them.

I love to hear their talk, although it's blurred,
But just the buzz, the hum, the lilt, the lovely laughter.
They don't yet understand how many of their children
Will be drained away by cities, nor do they know
The creamery will close, the general store, the school,
The post office, their neighbors grow more distant,
But all the grown-ups recognize that life's a shining thing,
However hard, and somehow, somewhere, someday
They will die, and they feel somewhat less alone
By sitting, standing, kneeling here beside
    The Big Stone.

Daylilies

What kind of music issues
From the brilliant trumpets
Of the daylilies? Is it pitched
So high only dogs can hear?
Birds? Butterflies? Bees?

Are these colorful megaphones
Howling like storm sirens
At the beetles and ants? *Take cover!*
Head for the cellar! Immediately!
No. Nothing so lovely—
Deep orange, buttercream—
Would sound so alarming.

We humans may not hear
The music of these tender trumpets,
But who can deny that we feel it,
A *basso profundo* so low
It makes everything tremble
Yet steadies us, too, like the ultrasound
From those long Buddhist horns in Tibet,
Rising right out of the bedrock.

Who wrote this music? Who knows?
All I know is that walking past
Our floral orchestra, I feel calmer
And friendly toward my neighbors,
Even the ones who annoy me!

Island River Redux

Here we go again, on a sweet retreat upriver,
Launching into the great quiet lying in wait all along
And only deepened now by the notable commotion
As a congregation of Canada geese shout their hymn
At our approach: *Rise Up! Rise Up! Rise Up and Go!*

How much of heaven can we ever know?
The cuddle and snuggle and rocking chair,
Ecstatic sex and its afterglow,
The circle of friends round a table,
The liquid passage of our canoe.

Political disaster, family despair
Dissolve in our wake as we go.
Sharp-shins chase the warblers south,
But white water lilies glow on black water,
Calmer than doves or Buddhist nuns.

What grains of wild rice remain
Show yellow, green, and blue maroon,
Reminding us of beads and quills.
They spray and sprinkle our packs as we pass.
Mallards and redheads dabble and dive.

The rice leaves droop like pennants
Of plenty here in this half-drowned land,
Where, long ago, an Ojibwe ancestor dreamed
His band would find food afloat on the water,
And hearing of this, they rose up and went.

Bog Root

Bog root, swamp stump, kale root, swede,
So called because commonly eaten
By cold country folk and our creatures—
Long-haired horses, cows, and pigs,
Who are happy enough, snuffling around
In frozen dirt and snowdrifts, to chomp
The cold purple shell of this vegetable
To get at the golden heart of the rutabaga—
That we may survive in our homes
Rather than die on the roads like so many beggars.

Are you sitting fat and sassy in the city?
Are you sipping exotic soups of Asia,
Buzzed on champagne, peppers and spice?
Hard times are coming, winter is coming,
The end of the world is on the way,
And therefore we celebrate bog root
Each year in Askov, Minnesota, the Rutabaga
Capital of the World. In Ithaca, New York,
We hold the International Rutabaga
Curling Championship and play with our food.

The bright spade sunk in black earth
Turns up rutabagas like buried shoes,
The heads of baby dolls we cradle
And carry away to our weathered sheds.
We skin them, we cut them in cubes
To simmer in soups and stews.
We mash them with carrots and spuds
And heap them in hills on our plates,
Annointed with butter, while cracks

Quickfracture the frozen lakes,
Booming like thunder. Inside, we're warm,
Thanks to bog root. We savor its tang
On the tongue, the tincture of cyanide
In the mellow mash by means of which we survive.

And so, while the well and all hell
Freeze over, as the bombs whistle down,
While the trees along the horizon
Explode into flame, come join with me, children,
Say: Give us this day our daily bog root.

Skyfall

Down the dusky glimmer of dawn,
snowfluff falls like ash
or stuffing come out of clouds,
or a heavy downdrift of cottonwood seeds,
milk froth, sea foam, a softness aloft,
almost appalling in dreamy descent,
ghosting the rooftops and trees,
yet lovely in lazy surrender and sift,
the gentle shock of an eyeful of skyfall
insisting we're lucky to live
where water can blossom in air
and our walkways fill
with infinitesimal flowers,
though the need to lift
and shift these dazzling drifts
is apt to put an ache in the back
it may take days to cure.

The Winter Vixen

Glancing through the glazed window,
I saw a fox, strawberry blonde,
Hunting among the white windrows.
Charmed by her neat black stocking-feet
As she rummaged below the bare lilacs,
I dropped what I was working on,
Curious what she'd find to eat.
Then I saw the second fox,
Half her size, hesitant, downright darling.
Could Mother find food for more than one?
The vixen nosed a stiffened starling
Out of a drift and crunched it down.
Frozen in place, I watched them go,
Padding over the crusted snow.

Redpoll Ruckus

Little Flitter, Finch of Winter,
Welcome to my thistle seeds.
Feed, my flighty friend,
Fulfill your thin, small self.
I like your black chin,
Your snub-nose bill,
Your brown offset
By the blush on your breast,
Not to mention, of course,
The raspberry dab
You wear as your crown.

Here you come, bang, in a bunch,
Looking for lunch, a handful
Flung in a flock, to glean
The ground beneath the weeds,
Or, one by one, you will
Cling to the feeder and eat
Seed after seed after seed.
Good grief! What greed!
Who knows what you need
To weather such crackling cold?
We'll weather this winter together.

A Beaver Lodge

I took the bridge and hiked uphill
Across the dreary clear-cut, then on
Through spruce where water spilled
And trickled from the beaver pond.

Climbing up the waist-high dam,
I watched the silver surface wink
With insect life. Mallards swam
In peace. I teetered on the brink

And cast a feathered spinnerbait
Among the trunks of naked trees.
I'd come too early or too late.
All I offered failed to please.

But how about those dimples there,
Just off that distant, sedgy point
Where beavers had their rustic lair?
I worked my way around the pond

In hopes of catching speckled trout—
Mucky footing, boughs to dodge,
Mosquitoes in their rising clouds—
Until I stood beside the lodge.

What a hodgepodge house to own!
As if a fright-wig eagle's nest
Had fallen here, but upside down.
Yet it had stood the winter's test.

And then I heard a gnawing sound,
The whimper of a beaver kit,
And grown-ups grumbling underground
So that I lost or found my wits

And stood there listening, stunned and dumb,
Absorbed by what I can't forget—
This life beyond my paltry one—
Thriving, secret, intimate.

Ghosts

How long ago did I step out
On that flat rock by the boggy bank
To take a break and pull the canoe
Up snug, out of the current?
It was early spring, the water cold.
I arched my back, let go a groan,
And smiled. No one around for miles.

But there was a flash, and another,
Back in the cedars. On a hunch and a hope,
I gave a soft whistle. I whistled,
And, lo, he showed, with, first,
A pale face in the cedar fronds,
And then, caving to curiosity,
Exposed himself with a swoop
To a bush in the bog: a gray jay,
Like a chickadee big as a robin.

Unlike their raucous cousins, the blues,
The grays keep still. If they call at all,
It's apt to be chatters and clicks
Or soft whistles. They resemble
Stuffed toys you wish you could
Offer some kids, but they're ghostly,
Arriving in silence, and often
Departing the same.

I confess I was foolishly proud and glad
To have whistled this one out of the woods,
And I loved the smooth of his swoop from one bush
To the next till he perched on the branch

Of a snag nearby and cocked his head
To consider me.

This jay was on his own but
Brought me flocks of memories
Of his kind in winter camps
Where I sat with friends on balsam boughs
Round crackling fires of cedar and spruce—
Not to mention the black-and-white
Photograph on the wall of my study
Of Joe, my ruddy-faced friend
Who shot himself dead in his thirties
But looks happy there in his twenties,
Standing before his snow-capped cabin
Many long miles north of nowhere,
Arm stretched out like a falconer's
And a gray jay perched on his hand.

This one gave me one last look and was gone.
I settled in the canoe and also moved along.
We left behind a low flat rock in the river
And a snag with a lone bare branch.

Catching Crappies Beneath a Pictograph

No walleyes yesterday, none so far today,
He trolls the river mindlessly, drinking in
The silence like a whisky called Serenity.
His paddle drips. The white-throats call.

How long since he's been back in here?
Eight years? Too long, god knows, too long.
And how far to the pictograph?
Just that much farther than he thought.

But now a whale of granite breaches
Bankside on the right, rising
Out of boggy ground. He slows
And drifts beneath the cliff,

Searching till it startles him.
Oh, yes. Hello. Figures on the rockface,
Facing him full-on, a man with something
In his hand—a knife, a club, a bow?

An antlered buck beside him, also
Facing out, and smaller, lower left,
A raven looking west. Such images
Have stuck to rock for centuries,

Painted by Ojibwe or the ones
Who came before. Iron oxide,
Mixed with fish oil, daubed on stone.
But how did they climb up so high—

Fifteen, twenty feet—to paint?
Sheer wall, the river right below.

Winter work? Just snowshoe up
A drift packed in against the cliff?

What's this? His rod is bowed
And pulsing at his thigh like blood
That surges in his heart. He snatches up
The handle, yanks, reels against

Resistance, there's a leap and splash,
And he shouts, "Bass!" He reels again
Against the dodging, diving fish,
Says, "Let me land him, Grandma."

And he does, he nets it, lifts. The fish
Explodes, baptizing him with waterdrops.
The man sits back, surprised,
And says its name: "A crappie? Crappie!"

The fish is a good foot long,
Oversized, glistening emerald, gold,
But better than treasure out here:
It can be eaten: Delectable flesh.

This beauty tied to a stringer,
The stringer to his canoe, he casts again
With a trembling hand. Two days out,
Time and the land are absorbing him.

The white man thanks his grandmother.
His feelings swim and soar.
He gazes at the pictograph.
He catches four fish more.

Swansong

Does it make any sense at all
To mention the soul on a day like today,
The lake deep silver, the sky a foggy gray,
Drizzle drifting through in waves,
And a single silver trout
Rattling the willow of my creel
As he suffocates for me? It's cold.
And quiet, the songbirds gone south,
Except for the *roik, roik* of a raven,
Followed by some trumpeting and thunder
As five swans at the far end of the lake
Decide, altogether, to get up and go.
I see the swans, like Jesus, can walk on water
As long as they keep running really hard,
Their wide wings colliding as they beat, beat, beat,
Beat and rise, and something lifts inside me
As they pass, shining like a snowstorm,
Laboring but taking flight.

The Moon Beside the Canoe

The full moon floats like a water lily
Beside the bow of the beached canoe.
I saw this years and years ago
With a friend who showed me through
This country, dead for decades now.
Back then, there were dozens of lakes to explore
And mysteries galore. Was God for real?
Was love? Could I make some words stand still?

I've seen the moon afloat like this
A hundred times since then.
I've seen my words pressed into books
Like keepsakes left behind. I've married
Twice, raised another man's kids,
And sometimes wondered why.
The wind blows where it will;
There's little we truly control.
No need to travel far these days:
A pond will float the moon.

I never met God, though I heard voices
In the wind and smelled perfume
In stands of balm of Gilead.
Strange feelings came to me at dawn
And dusk, but I learned to make do
With friends and a woman's touch.
I put my faith in granite and spruce
And the moon beside the canoe.

Here

The paddles dip at a steady clip;
    You can hear them hiss and drip.
The fog feels close, and as we go,
    All sounds sound soft and low.
We travel here with love and fear
    In a place that we revere,
Feeling most at home when we're alone
    Where loons and owls both moan.
Should we take a break? Let's try to make
    The far end of the lake,
Though it's hard to see through the mystery
    A single rock or tree.
We squint and peer. I'm glad we're here.
    I believe it's going to clear.

New Poems

(2022-2024)

Thinking Along with the *Tao Te Ching*

The snail shell, the ram's horn, the Milky Way
All partake of a mystery. Who can say
Where it starts or ends?
What we know for sure is that it bends.

Mowing

I believe a leaf of grass is no less
than the journeywork of the stars.

— *Walt Whitman: Song of Myself*

A little older, little weaker every year,
But, by god, I still can mow! A good thing, too.
Got a two-hour cut altogether—front yard,
Side yard, back yard, orchard,
And don't forget the boulevards.
Can you imagine the cost
If we had to hire that work out?
Many friends are dead, dying,
Or debilitated, yet I'm still out here
Mowing, wearing earmuffs like a pilot,
Flying around the yard, pushing Briggs
& Stratton up the hill like Sisyphus.

Once upon a time, I'd race through
The whole damn job in just one go.
These days, I need to break it up
In patches and recover in between,
But who's complaining? I am, I guess,
But keep it short because so many friends
Are fading. *The grass withers, the flower fades,*
When the breath of the Lord blows upon it;
Surely the people is grass. Meantime,
I'm reviving muscles that went slack
All winter. If I get sulky round the house,
My wife says, "Why don't you go mow?"

Well, okay, but if she hadn't planted
All these trees and flowers, I could buzz

Right through, but, no, I have to
Push and pull around them, careful,
Careful. It's a jungle out here.
Sixteen fruit trees in the orchard,
Where forty years ago was only fill.
Still, it's something, early summer,
When they all explode in bloom,
And her cherry pies? They're like
Eating Malbec or Cabernet, some serious
Consolation now that I can't drink.

And here's the thing. When you finally finish,
Look it over, comes a satisfaction. Sweet.
And I do some wacky stuff while going round
And round, the mower growling, growing
Heavy. I might sing, for instance:
We are climbing Jacob's ladder,
We are climbing Jacob's ladder,
We are climbing Jacob's ladder.
Soldiers—of the—cross. Crazy.
But I used to do that, mowing lawns
For money, twelve years old,
And that kid is with me while I sing.

Or I might recite a line or two by Robert Frost:
The fact is the sweetest dream that labor knows.
My long scythe whispered and left the hay to make.
Or, bumping over lumpy apples fallen in the grass,
I am overtired / Of the great harvest I myself desired.
If anyone could hear me, they'd believe that I was nuts,
But my muttering is swallowed by the mower's roar,
So I'm free to speak whatever dreamy drivel passes
Through my head because *Green grown the rashes, O!*

It gets worse. I'll talk directly to the grass:
"How did you jump up so high so fast?"
And trees: "Poor mountain ash! How we loved
Your orange and ruby leaves and how the waxwings
Feasted on your scarlet berries in late snows of spring.
But I see sapsuckers have drained you of your juice,
And so I need to take you down." I leave clover,
Whole banks of daisies, orange and yellow hawkweed,
Yet once they go to seed, I mow them down, shouting,
"Sorry, sorry!" I grieve, but only briefly, for I have found
That I believe not only in these fragile flags of hope,
But also the galactic web of roots and tender tendrils
underground.

Recalling What's-his-name

I haul a walleye, long as my forearm,
From weedy water into air, where
It glows and glitters, darkened gold,
A gift that goes on giving all week long as I keep on
Remembering, forgetting, then remembering again
Old What's-his-name from that nearly no-place town
Where several of my early years went up in smoke.

The thought of that fish will jab me
With a little jolt of joy, and I flash on
What's-his-name, a grown-up ne'er-do-well
Whose family owned a business selling peat
(Imagine! Selling dirt! Talk about a business plan!)
In which What's-his-name took little interest,
Though work meant pride and standing in those parts.

People shook their heads about that man
But also smiled at his slick escape from trappings
Of respectability, his jovial defiance
Of the laws of gravity. Drove a rattletrap
In contrast to his father's Cadillac.
Khaki clothes. Thirty-something. *What's his name?*
Michael? Marcus? Marvin? Mel? What the *hell?*

Is this the more-or-less essential
Amnesia growing old entails
Because no storage room remains?
Do we drop names into the trash
With no refresh to click, the same
As we pass on belongings to Goodwill?
For Pete's sake, what's his *name?*

I've fished my mind all week,
Remembering that dappled morning
In the woods along the Winnebago River,
One brother (which one?) my companion.
We heard a whoop, a scramble,
And out of the brush and bramble, laughing,
Here comes What's-his-name
With three bright walleyes on a stringer.
No. Walleyes from the Winnebago?
That slow meander through the corn and beans?
We gaped in awe. A wizard stood before us,
Khakis wet up to his knees. And now that appellation
Flashes like a fish that breaks the surface,
Leaps, and water sprays a rainbow in the sun:

Malcolm. Malcolm Colby.

A Field Full of Bobolinks

I reached the shore of our one salt lake
With hopes for what I'd found before,
More shorebirds than a man could count: ruddy
Turnstones turning stones, swirling phalaropes,
Avocets with cinnamon heads and graceful necks,
With black-and-white bodies and flashing wings,
With long blue legs and delicate upturned bills;
But a great storm had struck the area days before,
Tearing roofs off sheds, collapsing granaries,
Sending sheets of metal sailing into fields.
The birds had fled. The lake was bare.

I slumped, then extricated myself from the car,
Stretched . . . and heard forgotten but familiar
Music from the hayfield by the shore. Saw
Bobolinks! Old friends I hadn't seen for years.
I waded into waist-high grass and walked among them.
Chunky blackbirds swiped with white and patched
With buff on the back of the neck, hence
Their nickname: butterbirds. Killed off
By the millions, yet here they were, the little
Exhibitionists, still wearing their tuxedoes.

They swayed on long strong stems, then climbed the air,
Stood on wing-tips, cocked their heads back, sang.
Then sank. Ascended. Sang again. A fantastic spangle
Of liquid notes, which, when distant, sprinkled the sky
With sparkling sounds of bells the size of dew drops.
As the butterbirds rose and fell, I turned and turned
In that shower of sound and finally turned to go, fulfilled.

But paid—with the long diagonal drive across the state
And prinkling skin as I pinched, over the following hours,
A total of ten (count 'em) ten individual wood ticks
Creepy crawling up my neck. "Ick!" I hear some
Screen-bound city-slicker say, who hardly knows a sparrow
From a crow, "Who would do a thing like that
Just to hear a damn bird sing?" and have to ask,
"Have you ever seen a bobolink? Have you ever
Heard a bobolink sing? No? I didn't think so."

Eagle, Raven, Vulture, Deer

Instead of slacking off come night,
That nor'wester built. They huddled close,
Losing sleep to falling branches,
Loose guylines, the flimsy tent
Herky-jerking like some freaky
Mad balloon. Along toward dawn,
The wind made up their minds.
They could sneak along the river, but
The lake would be explosive, so
They'd have to hunker down.

Windbound, they hauled the tent
And all the gear down off the bluff
To find poor shelter in the woods
Behind a bulky boulder. Hunched there
Through the day, they nursed the stove
For soup and tea, tried to read,
And failed to nap inside the flapping tent.
The white noise rose and crackled
In the afternoon, and so they stumbled,
Dazed by the crescendo in the conifers,
Down along the riverbank to watch
The black spruce pitch and sway
Alarmingly, and then heard rifle shots
As tops began to snap and drop.
They stared—
Turned to each other, looked away,
Retreated to their boulder.

Sleep came fitfully that night,
But the wind did slowly ease.

They rose at dawn, surprised
To find the morning soft and calm,
So struck the tent, jammed things in packs,
And paddled strongly down the river,
Pumping hard to make the lake
Before the wind whipped up again.

At river's mouth, they stood on sand,
Dismayed. Although the wind was low,
The waves remembered yesterday,
Topped with white caps way, way out,
And broke with fury at their feet.
Still, they thought they knew a route—
If they could reach the islands, a quarter mile off,
They'd find less wild water, where
They could island hop to hit
The far west shore and use the lee
To slip down south and out.

Awkwardly, they boarded in the breakers.
"What should I do?" the wife yelled back.
"Just paddle hard!" her husband cried.
"Don't quit! This first will be the worst!"
And so it was. Once they dug past
The seething breakers, they could breathe,
And, gaining ground—or water, rather—
Leave their fear behind.

The islands grew. As they drew near,
They saw, there off the point, a skerry
Which barely cleared the waterline,
But there was movement. What
Was it on that slab of rock?

"Eagle! Eagle!" "Yes! And those
Black rocks are ravens."
Both proved true, as they approached,
Except, it seemed, one raven had
A buzzard's shocking bare red head.

How strange to see these raptors,
Dominators of the sky,
Abide each other peaceably.
They realized, then, the birds were banqueting
On something, which, as their canoe slid gently
On the swells, turned out
To be the carcass of a deer, not fresh
But washed up on the reef.
As they came closer, they could see
The naked ribs and hide, remains
To which the raptors bowed their heads,
Ripping strips and bits that they
Could not identify. Sheltered now,
They paddled gently. As they watched,
The birds began to eye them, too.

The eagle was the first to flare.
He spiraled up till feathers caught
And west wind sent him sailing.
The ravens went on eating, guardedly,
Until the boat came all too close,
Then also climbed the sky.
Vulture, though—its naked head
Evolved for groping wet recesses,
Cavities—continued feeding,
And the couple left it to its feast.

Back behind the islands, they found
Slacker water, so their progress west
Went easier, and then a place to pause.
A snack. A bit of cheese, handful of nuts,
A dark and chewy jerky strip,
Reminding them how they were kin
To birds of prey—and also carrion.

Why, then, were they so jubilant?
They felt the lift that food provides
When working out-of-doors. And then
The flush of complex gratitude:
No treetop had speared them, nor
Had breakers taken them, and they had seen
Raw hunger exorcised up close.
And been reminded, too,
How humans *in extremis*
Had been known to eat their own.

Yet here they were, well fed and strong,
Paddling and singing, sunlight slashing
Through the clouds, a vulture kiting
Overhead, the pair below
Still young enough to thrive
For many more long years, with luck,
Before the black-and-silver wings arrived.

Silence in the Auditorium

I'm haunted by that night
The white-haired poet asked
An audience of hundreds,
"How *do* we learn to die?"

That was years ago. This evening,
I walk out in the orchard where
The bird's nest in the bare birch tree
Slowly fills with snow.

> *In memoriam*
> *Robert Bly*

Coons

I'm in the cellar of the city,
Walking Chester Creek Ravine, and so,
Though it's a steamy day upstairs,
Down here, shaded by the greenery,
I'm cool as fog and drift along the trail,
Unthinking—a natural therapy
For worry warriors like me—
Admiring the rank slopes of thimbleberry,
Which offer white blossoms with the look
Of wild roses, inhaling *eau de pin rouge,*
While water sings the very best of songs:
"Isn't This Exactly What You Wanted?"

Abracadabra, out from behind
The trunk of a monumental white pine,
A foursome of small raccoons appears as one,
Shambling, stumbling, nudging and bumping
Each other, chirring and grumbling, muttering
        and mumbling,
Freezing me in place. My first thought: "Oh, my god,
For cute!" My second thought: "Thank you!"
My third thought, wary: "Where's their mom?"
For coons can attack. They're capable. The kits
Have stopped. *What's that?* they must be wondering.
Am I the first two-legged thing they've seen?
What am I? I'm not so sure, myself. But
I am filled with admiration of their silver fur,
The rings around their tails, the black bandito
Masks through which they see the world,
So much of which is so much
Taller than themselves. Thoughts of mother

Plus appreciation move me to applaud.
That does it. The sibling amalgamation
Turns as one, a mammalian amoeba,
And vanishes, retreating toward the creek,
Still muttering. What luck, I think, what luck!

Or so I'm feeling at the moment, but
Will I feel so keen when they are grown
And come looting garbage cans by night
Or popping up from city water drains?
Or how about that family of them nesting
In the neighbor's attic? What a nuisance!
And yet it *was* hilarious to look across and see
Half a raccoon looking round, relaxing
In the coon-sized hole they'd torn in the roof,
Like a soldier from the turret of a tank.

Still, I can't stop smiling and giving thanks
For this encounter. Truth is, I'm never more
Myself, whatever that is, never more relaxed
Than down here in this green ravine, away
From humanoids, their racket and machinery.
But now I must ascend the stairs, and so,
Regretfully, I pull on the cape of caution
And the tight, narrow mask with little eyeholes
To meet the world of men and women.

Big Band at Chester Bowl

Two hundred people were in the mood
To sprawl on the grass in Chester Bowl
For a sweet blast from the past. Stormy weather
Had come and gone, easing the heat
As the sun slid slowly down the sky.

A bank of trumpets and saxophones,
Piano, trombones, bass, and drums
Drew us into a musical swoon,
So you could have said we were in love
With the growl of the baritone sax,
The surprising meander on piano,
How the trumpets took off the top, dropped,
And the drums went swish and whack.

That was the year we choked on smoke
As half of Canada burned. Tearing up,
We sometimes sang *Smoke gets in your eyes*
For a laugh to lighten the atmosphere.
We hadn't meant to set the world on fire,
We didn't want to do it, we didn't want to do it,
But fools rushed in, and these foolish things
Were finally getting under our skin. Yet here
At last was a smoke-free, pleasant evening.

The band took a break, and a gaggle of kids
Across the creek raised a hullabaloo
On the run. They'd flushed a fox
Out of the woods, onto the footbridge, trapped,
As another gang flowed down the hill this side.
The face of the fox was alert, concerned.

What was she thinking? Oh, look at me now?
How come you do me like you do?
She hurried, scurried round a post,
Beneath the bridge, and doodley-doodley-doo.

Run, fox, run! Let's get away from it all.
Recall the horses, the hounds, the horns,
Even if you can't remember where or when.
Run, fox! Find your den. We're sorry now
For what we've gone and done.

The Song of the Veery

The song of the veery
  Starts up high, then spirals down
  Like a maple seed spins to the ground.
It says I am weary, weary, weary.

The song of the veery
  Is half a sigh and half a call.
  You hear it at evening most of all.
It says I am weary, weary, weary.

The song of the veery
  Is sweet but airy and slightly scary.
  You'd have to be crazy to call it merry.
It says I am weary, weary, weary.

The song of the veery
  Is half a whisper, half a cry,
  Reminding us we all must die.
It says I am weary, weary, weary.

Lupines

Somehow they always take me by surprise.
I'm speeding up the freeway, say,
Or turning down a gravel road, early
In mosquito season, midway into June,
And "Wow!" I'm shouting in the car,
"Lupines! There they are!" Already up
Three feet, in flocks, the ditch awash
In floods of pink, white, and royal blue,
Utterly exotic here where everything's gone green,
But unashamed, risen like Egyptian scepters
     from the earth.

They're phallic shapes, erect as rockets poised
To penetrate the sky, but where can they be going
Really? Where we all go in the end,
And soon, to ground, our common destination.
In the meantime, though, we have these gorgeous
Exclamation points that make us glad
We're here, right now!

     Moving closer,
We may see their petals look like pods,
Pockets, little pretty purses holding seeds.
So though the flowers fall, as flowers will,
Brown and wither and appear to disappear,
The seeds, roots, and rhizomes will remain,
Like buried fuses that will wait for spring
To burn and send up Roman candles.

And there's the rub. Lupine is not native
But invasive, and it spreads like fire

Sometimes smolders underneath a field of peat.
Log a patch of timber, and lupines storm
The ground. So beautiful they make us coo
But choke out native plants. So what?
Well, what if mammals, birds, and insects need
Those plants the lupines shouldered out?
Who likes buckthorn? Kudzu, anyone?
Then again, where'd *your* people come from?

I can't resist, swerve to the verge, park,
Clamber out, and fumble for my jackknife.
Approaching my quarry, I look both ways, for
Though this ditch is public, wouldn't you,
If you lived near, consider this choir of colors
Somehow yours? So I feel guilty, furtive,
But grab the stems of half a dozen whites,
Rarest of the colors here, and slash. Then pinks.
And then a great big bunch of almost purple blues.

A flower thief, I scope the road, hop in the car,
Toss the lupines on the side seat, and take off.
The lupines quiver as I drive the washboard,
Then settle with the smooth of asphalt. What a heist!
When I get home, I'll hand them to my wife,
Who'll say, "Oh, thank you! Oh, how lovely!"
Loving me and lupines, who got here god knows how.

The Monarch Man

There was a man who loved golf
And his brothers and hawks
And Mark Twain and football
And pretending to be Mark Twain
And baseball and his daughter
And teaching and reading and writing
And acting and eco-activism
And women, who loved him,
Though he confessed he'd learned
Through four divorces that
He could not give them what they wanted,
Which was someone other than he was,
Which was a man who loved canoes
And dogs, one old black lab especially,
And making jelly from his grapes
And giving this to friends and neighbors.
And Bob Dylan. Not to mention monarchs.

That is to say, the butterflies—large,
With orange wings with black veins
And a black body plus white spots.
This man collected fat green caterpillars,
Kept and fed them till they turned—you tell me how—
To light green chrysalises dotted gold,
Which hung from plants that he provided.
In time, these broke like bird eggs,
But not chicks but butterflies appeared.
Yet they were wet, and so they clung
To twigs or leaves until they dried,
Whereupon they flew. Who taught them how?
Who knows? But they were off to Mexico.

One time, one fall before he had a stroke
And later died, the Monarch Man's monarchs
Broke from their pupae, blossomed, and departed
As usual but for one stubborn chrysalis,
One late bloomer hanging on and on
Like some bud afraid of too much light
Till it finally popped. Looked fine, right
Splendid as it danced around the tent, and yet
The Monarch Man still worried, fretting to a friend
Over the phone: "He's too late. I know
The flyway, and I've calculated. His mates
Are all in Kansas, and the cold is going to catch him.
He'll just freeze if I release him here. So
I'm going to drive him down there. Listen.
You've got the key. Can you feed and water Cisco,
Take him for a walk? You know the drill.
I'll be back in two days, four days max.
Crazy? Crazy like a fox, my friend."

And so they went, the Monarch Man and his bright
Orange-and-black companion, blasting
          down the interstate—
Duluth, Des Moines, and onward, south
Southwest—the car packed with essentials:
Greenery, food, and water for the butterfly.
They spent one night in a motel. "Say,
I see you say no pets, but would you permit
A butterfly? I just have the one."

Somewhere east of Wichita, the Monarch Man
Saw what seemed orange poppies in a ditch,
But he knew better, pulled a U-turn,
Braked, wooed his winged passenger

Onto his finger, carefully stepped out,
And offered up, as if it were a falcon,
His monarch to the sky.

Two days to return, with stops for birding
Now and then. Once home, he held
A small impromptu party, where he looked
A bit bedraggled but smiled a wide smile
Of goofy and profound fulfillment
Made more pronounced by his mustache.

The Monarch Man has gone from us,
Leaving grief, delight, and wacky stories in his wake,
And a multitude of laughing, weeping friends—
Among them, several women who,
However much they loved him,
Could not live with him for long.

In memoriam
Phil Fitzpatrick

Among Ten Thousand Lakes, Just One Percent Are Deep and Cold Enough to Hold Lake Trout

for Grant Schluender

Shortly after ice-out, we found them
Fairly shallow, far side of the lake,
Below the cliff that rose above us
Like a thunderhead of rock.

Hooked, they fought us, not
By making runs but circling
And yanking down, *down*,
As if they wished to drown.

Led headfirst into the net,
They twisted—fish as dervish—
Diving, turning, writhing
Till our net was fraught with knots.

Such fierce hearts! And theirs
No bigger than our thumbnails!
We wearied them, snatched the lines,
And raised them into useless air.

Lake trout have a lunar look.
Rising from the dark, they're silver;
Yet lifted to the light, they glimmer
With a pale green wash.

Back at camp, we clubbed the fish
And laid them on a slope of moss,

Knelt, unsheathed our sharpened knives,
And—instead of praying, maybe—paused,

Took in the shimmer of their skin—
Like water dappled by the moon,
Silver water flecked by flakes of snow—
But then remembered we were men,

So bowed to work and opened one.
Its meat looked wonderful and strange,
As if that flesh were fruit. Blood orange.
And when we ate, we ate both sun and moon.

Song of the Small

As my granddaughter, so slight,
Who plays both violin and hockey,
Walks the walk and climbs the steps,
Her blonde hair shining, though the day is gray,
Her smile bright, her high voice clear,
She's bubbling with news of all
That she's already seen and done.

Meanwhile, a wren so small
That you could hold it in your hand
If you could somehow catch it,
Writes excited scribbles in the air,
Singing its own significant song.

None of this appears on the nightly news
Of what's purportedly important.

Afterword

When Norton Stillman invited me to assemble a book of nature poems from my past work, I was pleased, having considered that idea, myself, and listened to friends suggest the same. But when a friend asked what I was up to, and I told her I was putting together a book of nature poems, she said, "Oh. I prefer poems about people." I understand. People are interested in people. Kids are interested in kids. Dogs are interested in dogs. So be it. But "the other" also has its fascinations, while our narrow self-interest has brought us to the brink of self-destruction.

What *is* nature anyhow? We talk as if we knew. Here's my favorite dictionary definition: "the sum total of all things in time and space." Hilarious! That leaves room for a poem on any topic! But what we most often mean by "nature" seems to be plants, animals, and landscapes apart from humans and our products. It's a useful distinction but very far from the whole truth and can also be a deadly one, which we are learning as we suffer the consequences of believing in the extra-special status of our species. Indigenous people generally knew better. So did the poet Isaiah, with his awful, beautiful metaphor: "The grass withers, the flower fades; / Surely the people is grass." With the science of ecology, we moderns are finally catching on. Let's hope we're not too late.

In any case, there's always at least *one* person in any nature poem—the poet. The first-person pronoun may be absent, but *someone* chose this subject, someone made these observations, someone gave them voice. Even with a more-or-less objective description of a rock, we sense the presence of an author. And the author is a mammal with a highly complex language compared to other animals yet still an animal. Therefore, we might argue, every poem's a nature poem. But then the term "nature poem" loses all its meaning. Maybe it should. It occurs to me that in all the nature poems I've written, it's doubtful that "nature" is a word I've ever used.

Choosing poems for any collection and arranging them in what seems the most effective order is both a challenge and a pleasure. In this instance, I surveyed the poems in eight books from a lifetime of writing and found at least a third of them might be considered "nature poems." Of these, many included people and their products. Some were set in cities. In one of them, a sonnet, nature as we normally think of it was barely mentioned until it made a dramatic entrance in the last two lines. The crucial principle for me, once it rose to consciousness, was this: a nature poem is one in which the non-human world plays at least as important a role in the poem as people and their products.

Even with this principle as guide, of course, many choices remained. One large but relatively easy decision was to narrow the field by restricting my selections to poetry set in my home territory—the Upper Midwest and western Ontario. Geography, I wagered, would help the book cohere. This meant sacrificing poems from other places; but making a good book is about leaving things out as much as putting things in. *Cotton Grass* would be a Northern book.

Among the few poems set in regions from outside my home area, I chose to include two from a cycle called "Cow Calls in Dalarna" (Sweden) and selections from another, "The Reindeer Camps" (Siberia), as samples of my interest in Northern herding cultures. I also included "Lost in *Antarctica,*" a poem about Eliot Porter's photographs of that continent, which, as the poem says, "is so far south of south / Every vantage point looks north." Such work seemed so closely related to the rest that leaving it out would be a mistake.

Despite the efforts of my generation, the audience for poetry remains relatively small and its effect on society seems modest. And yet I've hoped my nature poems might serve among what William Stafford called the "millions of intricate moves" to arrive at justice—in this case, a way of living in and with the natural world rather than destroying it—and ourselves—with unbridled cleverness, arrogance, and greed. The longer I lived with the poem "Cotton Grass," the more that plant—growing in out-of-the-way places yet lovely to discover, self-propagating, and surprisingly tenacious—the more that plant seemed symbolic of poetry itself.

After half a century of enjoyable, exhausting effort putting poems in front of people—publishing, doing readings and interviews, touring with musicians, sending poems out to ride the skies on radio waves, producing verse plays, giving talks and workshops, teaching classes, embarrassing myself with self-promotion—the process by which poems find a route to readers' hearts remains, to me, a mystery. But *that* it happens and alters lives in ways both large and small—of that, I'm certain sure. For people sometimes write or introduce themselves to say as much of something that I've written. And the granite rock of evidence on which I stand is that poetry found, changed, and strengthened me.

When I was nineteen, I borrowed a friend's canoe, paddled and portaged along the Northern border, and sneaked across to a lake with islands and plenty of pike, where I spent half the summer sharing a trapper's shack with a couple of mice. The packs were heavy, but I added a book of poems to their heft—*The Back Country* by Gary Snyder. I enjoyed the poems for their own sake, but they also affirmed what I was doing out there by myself and helped me see—and see into and beyond what I was seeing.

Experience has taught me to keep my expectations low when it comes to the reception of a book of poems. I'm still hanging onto one fantasy for this one, though: that, at the last minute, some young hiker or paddler, heading out into the quiet, slips a copy of *Cotton Grass* into a pack and finds it well worth the added weight.

Bart Sutter
Duluth, Minnesota

January 15, 2024
8 below zero

Acknowledgments

I am grateful to the publishers of my earlier books from which poems were selected for inclusion in *Cotton Grass.*

Credit: Barton Sutter, poems from *Pine Creek Parish Hall and Other Poems* are copyright © 1985 by Barton Sutter. All are reprinted with the permission of Sandhills Press, Inc.

Credit: Barton Sutter, poems from *The Book of Names: New and Selected Poems, Farewell to the Starlight in Whiskey,* and *The Reindeer Camps and Other Poems* are copyright © 1993, 2004, 2012 by Barton Sutter. All are reprinted with the permission of The Permissions Company, LLC on behalf of BOA Editions, Ltd., boaeditions.org.

Credit: Barton Sutter, poems from *Chester Creek Ravine: Haiku, Nordic Accordion: Poems in a Scandinavian Mood,* and *So Surprised to Find You Here* are copyright © 2015, 2018, 2022 by Barton Sutter. All are reprinted with the permission of Nodin Press

My thanks, also, to the editors of these publications in which some of the new poems first appeared:

The Raven's Perch: "Coons," "A Field Full of Bobolinks"
Twin Ports Perceptions: "Big Band at Chester Bowl"
Valparaiso Poetry Review: "Song of the Small"

Thanks to Jamie Newton, several of the more recent poems were broadcast by KURU radio, Silver City, New Mexico.

My love and gratitude to the Lake Superior region, where I've been most at home. Praise to those who established the Superior National Forest and the Boundary

Waters Canoe Area Wilderness and to all those who work to sustain them, including government employees, who don't get thanked enough.

Daily thanks to my late parents, who, from the first, encouraged my affection for the natural world. My cousin David L. Pearson lit my interest in birding when I was nine. My uncles Melvin Sutter and Ray Koep gave me dangerous ideas about the pleasures of fishing. Encountered early, the books of Sigurd Olson, with pen-and-ink drawings by Francis Lee Jaques, gave me one important compass reading for my life.

These poems have been motivated in part by affection and gratitude for my primary companions in the woods and on the water: my brother Ross, Joe Huff, Dexter Thue, Jim Lodahl, Jim Johnson, Grant Schluender, Walt Prentice, Cheryl Dannenbring, and my wife, Dorothea Diver. That my daughters—Lilo Schluender and Bettina Stuecher—camp, canoe, hike, and ski with zest and skill is a source of pride and inspiration.

I owe ongoing gratitude to family and friends for tolerating my slow, impractical, daydreamy ways, for criticism and encouragement. These people were especially helpful with the new poems: Dan D'Allaird, Cheryl Dannenbring, Dorothea Diver, John Herold, Jim Johnson, Ilze Mueller, Howard Nelson, and Walt Prentice.

The retrospective gaze over a lifetime of writing required by this book moves me to thank, in particular, poets Howard Nelson and the late Philip Dacey for our long friendships, maintained almost exclusively by exchanging letters, poems, and books. How strange that these two friendships-at-a-distance have proved to be so crucial.

A word of thanks to Jean Replinger, a maven of outdoor education who taught me and many others to cross-country ski when we were young, and also gave encouragement to those of us who later became involved in projects dedicated to the natural world. I also want to offer gratitude to my first wife, Annette Atkins, for her belief, encouragement, and support in our early, often difficult years together as young writers.

This may seem foolish or presumptuous, but I want, here toward the end of my life, to name some famous names. I don't mean to "drop" them but to thank and honor them. Some readers, too, taken by poems in *Cotton Grass,* might appreciate a list "for further reading." These are the "nature poets"—all of them dead but one—who have meant the most to me, both as a writer and a man: Basho, Buson, Issa, John Clare, Walt Whitman, Gerard Manley Hopkins, D. H. Lawrence, Robinson Jeffers, Robert Frost, Theodore Roethke, Elizabeth Bishop, Maxine Kumin, David Wagoner, Robert Bly, James Wright, Galway Kinnell, Donald Hall, Gary Snyder, Ted Hughes, Mary Oliver, Seamus Heaney.

Finally, my thanks to Norton Stillman and John Toren of Nodin Press, for welcoming this collection and ushering it into print with care.

About the Author

Bart Sutter received the Minnesota Book Award for poetry with *The Book of Names,* for fiction with *My Father's War and Other Stories,* and for creative non-fiction with *Cold Comfort: Life at the Top of the Map.* Among other honors, he has won a Jerome Foundation Travel & Study Grant (Sweden), a Loft-McKnight Award, a Bush Foundation Fellowship, and the Bassine Citation from the Academy of American Poets. Sutter has written for public radio, he has had four verse plays produced, and for more than thirty years, he performed as one half of The Sutter Brothers, a poetry-and-music duo. Bart Sutter lives on a hillside overlooking Lake Superior with his wife, Dorothea Diver.